Whitehead's categoreal scheme

and other papers

by

R. M. MARTIN

MARTINUS NIJHOFF

THE HAGUE

WHITEHEAD'S CATEGOREAL SCHEME
AND OTHER PAPERS

WHITEHEAD'S CATEGOREAL SCHEME
AND OTHER PAPERS

by

R.M. MARTIN

MARTINUS NIJHOFF - THE HAGUE - 1974

ISBN 90 247 1659 4

PRINTED IN BELGIUM

For
Charles and Dorothy Hartshorne,
with love and gratitude.

"MULTA DIES, VARIIQUE LABOR MUTABILIS AEVI,
RETTULIT IN MELIUS, MULTOS ALTERNA REVISENS
LUSIT, ET IN SOLIDO RURSUS FORTUNA LOCAVIT."

TABLE OF CONTENTS

PREFACE

The philosophical papers comprising this volume range from process metaphysics and theology, through the phenomenological study of intentionality, to the foundations of geometry and of the system of real numbers. New light, it is thought, is shed on all these topics, some of them being of the highest interest and under intensive investigation in contemporary philosophical discussion. Metaphysicians, process theologians, semanticists, theorists of knowledge, phenomenologists, and philosophers of mathematics will thus find in this book, it is hoped, helpful materials and methods.

The categoreal scheme of Whitehead's *Process and Reality* is discussed rather fully from a logical point of view in the first paper [I] in the light of the author's previous work on the logico-metaphysical theory of events. The clarification that results is thought to provide a new depth and precision to the problem of interpreting one of the most difficult books in the recent history of metaphysics and cosmology.

A detailed examination of some aspects of Hartshorne's recent *Creative Synthesis and Philosophic Method* is given in II. This book is perhaps the most significant work on process philosophy since *Process and Reality* itself, and its logical underpinnings thus merit a full critical discussion.

On the basis of I and II the Whiteheadian theory of God is examined in III and a kind of "rational reconstruction" for it provided. In recent years process philosophy has quickly developed into a process theology. It is thought to be of as much interest therefore to attempt to present adequate logico-metaphysical foundations for the one as for the other.

The fourth paper is devoted to an *explication de texte* of one of the most difficult passages in Whitehead, namely, the crucial pages in

Process and Reality devoted to the notion of a *coordinate division*. This notion is of fundamental importance in the theory of extensive connection, which in turn paves the way for Whitehead's account of geometry, space, and time.

In V another of the most difficult passages in Whitehead, the Chapter "Abstraction" in *Science and the Modern World,* is examined closely. This is probably the most important passage in Whitehead on the doctrine of eternal objects and of how they are related amongst themselves.

The net result of these papers on Whitehead and Hartshorne is to show that their concerns are much closer to those of contemporary analytic philosophers than is commonly supposed. At the same time it is evident that their basic insights require further clarification and elaboration in the light of newer developments in logic.

VI is devoted to the foundations of what is called '*protogeometry*'. The use of this word is suggested by Paul Lorenzen's use of 'proto-physics'—the word, not the content. In protogeometry fundamental notions are characterized in terms of which the special geometries may be developed each in its own way. Protogeometry is a part of event metaphysics, just as arithmetic is, and in this paper it is shown explicitly how. The methods used are a natural outgrowth of Whitehead's work on coordinate divisions.

Some aspects of *Fitch's* philosophical and cosmological views are discussed in VII, especially as concerns mathematics and the good. In important respects these views are close to those of Whitehead. On the basis of the material of VI a new approach to the *foundations of the real-number system* is outlined, supplanting Fitch's own more constructivistic procedures.

VIII is devoted to a quite rigorous logical analysis of the celebrated *ontological argument* of St. Anselm. Although this argument has attracted considerable recent attention on the part of philosophic logicians, no one seems to have probed very deeply the linguistic forms needed for an exact statement.

Various topics covered in *Bocheński's* important and pioneering work, *The Logic of Religion,* are reflected upon at some length in IX both critically and constructively. Bocheński's book seems to be the only one of its kind and merits a most careful discussion.

In X a sympathetic "rational reconstruction" of the *Husserl-Gurwitsch* theory of *intentionality* is given in semantico-pragmatical terms. This reconstruction is thought to be of interest in showing how much more intimately the phenomenological theory of intentionality is related to recent developments in philosophic logic than is commonly supposed.

The author is indebted to the National Science Foundation, Grants GS-273 and GS-3069, to the Vaughn Foundation, to the Universität Hamburg, and to New York and Northwestern Universities for support of the work presented in this volume. Also thanks are due the Editors of *Philosophy and Phenomenological Research*, the *International Philosophical Quarterly*, *The Southern Journal of Philosophy*, *Diálogos*, and *The Monist* for permission to rework or borrow material originally appearing in the pages of those journals.

AN APPROXIMATIVE LOGICAL STRUCTURE FOR WHITEHEAD'S CATEGOREAL SCHEME

"INVENI PORTUM : SPES ET FORTUNA VALETE :
NIL MIHI VOBISCUM : LUDITE NUNC ALIIS."

1

It should not be forgotten that Whitehead was a professional mathematician for most of his academic life and that he spent ten years or so collaborating with Bertrand Russell on *Principia Mathematica*. Logico-mathematical methods and procedures must have become thoroughly ingrained in his habits of thought by the time the later metaphysical works were written. The suggestion that Whitehead may have forgotten these methods or no longer trusted them must surely be in error. For him, it would seem, to think at all was to think mathematically. Even in *Process and Reality* [1] it is interesting to discern mathematical or quasi-mathematical notions, definitions, and statements creeping in almost unawares on every page. The great categoreal scheme of this book, in fact, it will be contended, may be viewed as a kind of logico-mathematical system in disguise. It is the purpose of this present paper, in any case, to take a few first, tentative steps towards substantiating such a claim.

It might be objected that Whitehead himself, in the opening chapter, writes (p. 12) that "philosophy has been misled by the example of mathematics; and even in mathematics the statement of the ultimate logical principles is beset with difficulties, as yet insuperable." Also, (pp. 11-12) "philosophy has been haunted by the unfortunate notion that its method is dogmatically to indicate premises which are severally clear, distinct, and certain; and to erect upon those premises a deductive system of thought." On the other hand, Whitehead emphasizes that the categoreal scheme must be "coherent" and "logical," and that (p. 5) "the term 'logical' has its ordinary meaning, including

---

[1] (The Macmillan Co., New York : 1939), esp. pp. 27-45.

'logical' consistency, or lack of contradiction, the definition of con-structs in logical terms, the exemplification of general logical notions in specific instances, and the principles of inference." Also (p. 13) "the use of the categoreal scheme ... is to argue from it boldly and with rigid logic. The scheme should therefore be stated with the utmost precision and definiteness, to allow of such argumentation." ... "Speculative boldness (p. 25) must be balanced by complete humility before logic, and before fact."

There is no conflict between these two types of statements if it is recognized (p. 12) that "the accurate expression of the final generalities is the goal of discussion and not its origin" and that "metaphysical categories ... are tentative formulations of the ultimate generalities." Thus even tentative statements are to be expressed "with the utmost precision and definiteness" and with "complete humility before logic." If "the logician's alternative, true or false" is applied to the scheme of philosophic categories regarded "as one complex assertion ... the answer must be that the scheme is false. The same answer must be given to a like question respecting the existing formulated principles of any science." The categoreal scheme is put forward rather in a provisory way, to be improved upon by further reflection, better formulation, deeper insight, and discovery of further facts, scientific laws, and so on. Thus it is not "dogmatically" contended that the items of the categoreal scheme are "severally clear, distinct, and cer-tain." Such a contention would indeed be unfortunate, and has been abandoned for the most part even in mathematics. Not only the "diffi-culties, as yet insuperable" that infect *Principia Mathematica* (as Whitehead noted, p. 12, footnote 3), but also the presence now of various kinds of set-theoretic alternatives, Gödel's incompleteness theorem, the Löwenheim-Skolem theorem, various intuitionistic and constructivistic systems—all of these militate against any dogmatically certain rendition of the fundamental notions of mathematics. White-head's strictures against mathematics, written before 1929, are based upon an inadequate conception of its foundations and are no longer applicable.

2

Let us try to sketch the kind of logical underpinning that seems needed for the whole cosmological scheme of *Process and Reality*, without however even a hint as to dogmatic finality of statement.

The effort is made to stay fairly close to the letter of what Whitehead writes, but even so, much "interpretation" must be allowed, much reading between the lines, much straightening out of minor matters for purposes of achieving rigor and system, and so on. The final result, it is hoped, will not be too far off as a first approximation.

Whitehead was thoroughly familiar with the theory of types in the ramified version of the first edition of *PM*. The difference between the ramified and the later simplified version seems irrelevant for present purposes. Perhaps if the distinction between the two versions were to be disregarded, some surreptitious distortion would creep in, but this seems unlikely. Thus 'the theory of types' here refers only to the simplified version, even though its formulation came several years after the publication of *PM* itself.

In V below, concerning the chapter "Abstraction" in *Science and the Modern World*, it will be argued that there is a close formal affinity between the "analytical character of the realm of eternal objects" and the theory of types. This affinity seems so close as to suggest that Whitehead was perhaps presupposing a type theory in *Process and Reality* itself. However, there is little in this later work to substantiate this, almost all the evidence for it being in the "Abstraction" chapter. In *Process and Reality* the "analytical character of the realm of eternal objects" seems to play scarcely any explicit role at all. Even so, it is no doubt there implicitly in some fashion.

One way of attempting to characterize the logic underlying *Process and Reality* would therefore be to presuppose type theory explicitly. Indeed, it seems that this could be done without too much difficulty. Type theory has its own complications, however, mainly notational.[2] Each variable and non-logical constant must be given two numeral tags, one for its type and one for its degree. Thus 'x_m^n' could be a variable or proper name of n-th type and of m-th degree, that is, for an m-adic relation of type n. If all relations are regarded as homogeneous in the sense that all the arguments are of the same type, then technical devices for raising type are needed to handle non-homogeneous relations. Considerable notational complication results. To avoid this, it seems better not to presuppose a type theory except insofar as it may be built up within the context of a broader set theory.

---

[2] See V below. Cf. also R. Carnap, *Introduction to Symbolic Logic* (Dover, New York : 1958), Chapter C, and the author's *Truth and Denotation* (University of Chicago Press, Chicago : 1958), Chapter VI.

Thus it will be more propitious here to presuppose a set theory of some kind, perhaps that of Zermelo or some sufficiently similar alternative. The formulation below, in this merely approximative reconstruction, will not be such as to depend upon the special form of set theory used. Thus no axioms will be provided, and the set theory will be left "naive." This procedure seems not unreasonable at the present stage. More refined formulations would depend most intimately, however, upon the niceties of the axiomatic set theory presupposed.

3

As good a way to begin as any is to reflect straitaway upon the Category of the Ultimate, the eight Categories of Existence, the twenty-seven Categories of Explanation, the nine Categoreal Obligations, and the theory of Extensive Connection. These provide the heart of the system, of which all else is an elaboration. The Category of the Ultimate is the least definite, and it will be better to reflect upon the others first.

Among the eight Categories of Existence, it will be recalled, "actual entities and eternal objects stand out with a certain extreme finality." Presumably entities of these two kinds are to be taken as *values for variables*, and the other kinds of entities, which have "a certain intermediate character," are to be regarded somehow as partaking of both.[3] Thus *prehensions* may be regarded merely as a special kind of actual entity. Likewise *subjective forms* may be regarded in turn as certain sets or kinds of prehensions, and *propositions* as constructs involving actual occasions as subjects and a complex eternal object as predicate. *Nexūs* are "sets" of occasions, as Whitehead explicitly states, interrelated among each other in a certain way. *Multiplicities* and *contrasts* are less fundamental and can no doubt be handled also as suitable sets.

Let 'e', 'e'', and so on, and 'e_1', 'e_2', and so on, now be variables taking actual occasions as values. And let 'α', 'β', and 'γ', with or without primes or numerical subscripts, be variables for eternal objects. In addition all manner of sets, relations, sets of sets, and so

---

[3] On being values for variables, see the author's *Belief, Existence, and Meaning* (New York University Press, New York : 1969), Chapter II.

on, may be used without qualms as provided in the underlying set theory. Such notions are indispensable for Whitehead the mathematician and their use by him quā speculative philosopher is presumably beyond question. Perhaps sets, sets of sets, and so on, may themselves be regarded as eternal objects, but for the moment this need not be assumed.

As variables in the naive underlying set theory, let 'μ' and 'ν', again with or without primes or numerical subscripts, be used. In effect then these are variables for sets of actual occasions, sets of eternal objects, sets of prehensions, and so on, depending upon the context. Also suitable set constants, proper names of specific sets, may be introduced as needed, either as primitive or defined. Let 'ϵ' as is customary be the sign for the relation of membership, so that '$e \in \mu$' and '$\alpha \in \mu$' express respectively that the occasion e is a member of μ and that the eternal object α is of member of μ.

Prehensions are to be handled as special kinds of actual entities, in the following way. Let

$$\text{'}e_1 \text{ Prhd } e_2\text{'}$$

express, primitively, that the actual entity e_1 prehends physically the actual entity e_2. 'Prhd' here is a primitive relational constant for the dyadic relation of physical prehending. A prehension is any particular act or occasion or instance of a prehending. More particularly, a physical prehension is an act or occasion describable by saying that it is an "e_1-bearing-Prhd-to-e_2" occasion. Fortunately a notation for these is forthcoming in *event logic*.[4] (Conceptual prehension will be provided for in a moment by allowing 'Prhd' also to be significant in other contexts.)

Where 'e_1 Prhd e_2' holds let

$$\text{'}\langle e_1, \text{Prhd}, e_2 \rangle e\text{'}$$

express that e is an e_1-bearing-Prhd-to-e_2 act or occasion, that is, that e is a prehending of e_2 by e_1. The theory of this notation is spelled out, to some extent anyhow, in event logic.

An expression of the form '$\langle e_1, \text{Prhd}, e_2 \rangle$' is an *event-descriptive* predicate. The application of such a predicate to an event e as argument enables us to express that e is such and such a *kind* of event, it enables us to *describe* e, not fully of course, but only partially in the

[4] See *Belief, Existence, and Meaning*, Chapter IX, the author's *Logic, Language, and Metaphysics* (New York University Press, New York : 1971), Chapter VII and VIII, and *Events, Reference, and Logical Form* (The Catholic University of America Press, Washington : 1974).

way in which any predicate partially describes an entity to which it applies. The admission here of event-descriptive predicates is most important in providing a suitable notation for prehensions.

There are two "species" of prehensions, according to CE(xii), the twelfth Category of Explanation, positive and negative. Let 'Pos' and 'Neg' be primitives significant in the contexts

$$\text{'}e \,\epsilon\, \text{Pos'} \text{ and } \text{'}e \,\epsilon\, \text{Neg'},$$

respectively expressing that e is a positive prehension and that e is a negative one. Let

'$\langle e_1,{}^+\text{Prhd},e_2\rangle e$' abbreviate '$(\langle e_1,\text{Prhd},e_2\rangle e \,\cdot\, e \,\epsilon\, \text{Pos})$',

'$\langle e_1,{}^-\text{Prhd},e_2\rangle e$' abbreviate '$(\langle e_1,\text{Prhd},e_2\rangle e \,\cdot\, e \,\epsilon\, \text{Neg})$',

'$e_1 \,{}^+\text{Prhd}\, e_2$'   abbreviate '$(Ee)\langle e_1,{}^+\text{Prhd},e_2\rangle e$',

and

'$e_1 \,{}^-\text{Prhd}\, e_2$'   abbreviate '$(Ee)\langle e_1,{}^-\text{Prhd},e_2\rangle e$'.

The definienda read, respectively, 'e is a positive physical prehending of e_2 by e_1', 'e is a negative physical prehending of e_2 by e_1', 'e_1 physically prehends e_2 positively', and 'e_1 physically prehends e_2 negatively'.

The following principles clearly obtain.

$(e_1)(e_2)(e_1 \,\text{Prhd}\, e_2 \equiv (Ee)\langle e_1,\text{Prhd},e_2\rangle e)$,

$(e_1)(e_2)(e_1 \,{}^+\text{Prhd}\, e_2 \equiv (Ee)\langle e_1,{}^+\text{Prhd},e_2\rangle e)$,

$(e_1)(e_2)(e_1 \,{}^-\text{Prhd}\, e_2 \equiv (Ee)\langle e_1,{}^-\text{Prhd},e_2\rangle e)$,

$(e_1)(e_2)(e)(\langle e_1,\text{Prhd},e_2\rangle e \supset (e \,\epsilon\, \text{Pos} \,v\, e \,\epsilon\, \text{Neg}))$,

$(e)(e \,\epsilon\, \text{Pos} \equiv \sim e \,\epsilon\, \text{Neg})$,

$\sim (Ee)(Ee')(Ee_1)(Ee_2)(\langle e,\text{Prhd},e'\rangle e_1 \,\cdot\, \langle e,\text{Prhd},e'\rangle e_2 \,\cdot\, e_1 \,\epsilon\, \text{Pos} \,\cdot\, e_2 \,\epsilon\, \text{Neg})$.

4

In addition to prehensional sentences of the form '$e \,\text{Prhd}\, e'$', suitable forms for *conceptual* prehensions are needed in accord with CE(xi). "Prehensions of actual entities. ... are termed 'physical prehensions'; and prehensions of eternal objects are termed 'conceptual prehensions'." It might be thought that '$e \,\text{Prhd}\, \alpha$' would be a suitable form for handling conceptual prehensions. Such a form, however, would turn out to be too "abstract." Occasions do not prehend eternal objects *simpliciter* but only *relative to* the occasions in which they may ingress. Thus '$e \,\text{Prhd}\, \alpha,e'$' may be introduced to express that actual occasion e prehends the eternal object α as (potentially or actually) ingressing in (or relative to its potential or actual ingression in) occasion e'. Similarly 'e Prhd α,e_1,e_2' may express that e bears Prhd to the dyadic relational eternal object α as holding potentially or actually between occasions e_1 and e_2. And similarly for more complex forms involving triadic-relational eternal objects, and so on. The usefulness, indeed the indispensability, of these forms will become clear in connection with the Categoreal Obligations.

To say that $\langle e_1,\text{Prhd},\alpha,e_2\rangle e$, where a predicate of the kind available in event logic is used, is to say that e is a conceptual prehension by e_1 of α with respect to e_2.

For convenience and to avoid unnecessary technicality, let it be assumed hereafter that k (or k) is the degree of the primitive eternal-object constant or variable of highest degree admitted. This assumption will help to simplify several statements below. Thus

$$\text{'}e \text{ Prhd } \alpha,e_1,\ldots e_k\text{'}$$

will be the atomic form of greatest length to be met with for handling conceptual prehensions. This limitation does not mean that eternal objects of degree $> k$ cannot be handled, but only that expressions for them are to regarded as defined rather than as primitive.

In familiar fashion, let now

$$\text{'}\langle e,{}^{+}\text{Prhd},\alpha,e_1,\ldots,e_n\rangle e'\text{'}$$
$$\text{'}\langle e,{}^{-}\text{Prhd},\alpha,e_1,\ldots,e_n\rangle e'\text{'}$$
$$\text{'}e \text{ }{}^{+}\text{Prhd } \alpha,e_1,\ldots,e_n\text{'},$$

and

$$\text{'}e \text{ }{}^{-}\text{Prhd } \alpha,e_1,\ldots,e_n\text{'}$$

be defined for each n such that $1 \leq n \leq k$. Clearly then

$(e)(e')(\alpha)(e \text{ Prhd } \alpha,e' \equiv (Ee')(\langle e,\text{Prhd},\alpha,e'\rangle e'')$,
$(e)(e')(\alpha)(e \text{ }{}^{+}\text{Prhd } \alpha,e' \equiv (Ee'')\langle e,{}^{+}\text{Prhd},\alpha,e'\rangle e'')$,

and so on.

Also the following principles of identity obtain.

$(e_1)(e_2)(e)(e')((\langle e_1,{}^{+}\text{Prhd},e_2\rangle e \cdot \langle e_3,{}^{+}\text{Prhd},e_4\rangle e') \cdot e = e') \supset (e_1 = e_3 \cdot e_2 = e_4))$,
$(e_1)(e_2)(e)(e')(\alpha)(\beta)((\langle e_1,{}^{+}\text{Prhd},\alpha,e_2\rangle e \cdot \langle e_3,{}^{+}\text{Prhd},\beta,e_4\rangle e') \cdot e = e') \supset (e_1 = e_3 \cdot \alpha = \beta \cdot e_2 = e_4))$,

and so on. And similarly for negative prehensions. (Under suitable restrictions the converses of these perhaps also hold.)

Let 'EO^1' designate the set of all monadic eternal objects, 'EO^2' that of dyadic ones, and so on. '$\alpha \in$ EO^n' thus expresses primitively that α is an n-adic eternal object. Then

'$\alpha \in$ EO' may abbreviate '($\alpha \in$ EO^1 v $\alpha \in$ EO^2 v $\ldots$ v $\alpha \in$ EO^k)'.

Clearly the following principles now hold.

$(e)(e_1)(\alpha)(e')(\langle e,\text{Prhd},\alpha,e_1\rangle e' \supset \alpha \in \text{EO}^1)$,

$(e)(e_1)(e_2)(\alpha)(e')(\langle e,\text{Prhd},\alpha,e_1,e_2\rangle e' \supset \alpha \in \text{EO}^2)$,

and so on, as well as

$(e)(\alpha)(e')(e \text{ Prhd } \alpha,e' \supset \alpha \in \text{EO}^1)$,

$(e)(\alpha)(e_1)(e_2)(e \text{ Prhd } \alpha,e_1,e_2 \supset \alpha \in \text{EO}^2)$,

and so on. Also

$(\alpha)(\alpha \in \text{EO}^1 \text{ v } ... \text{ v } \alpha \in \text{EO}^k)$,

$(\alpha)(\alpha \in \text{EO}^i \supset \sim \alpha \in \text{EO}^j)$, for $i \neq j$, $1 \leq i \leq k$, and $1 \leq j \leq k$.

EO is the universal set of eternal objects. In similar fashion. 'AO' may be defined as the universal set of actual entities or occasions. '$e \in \text{AO}$' abbreviates '$e = e$'.

Also 'Prhn' may be defined for the set of all prehensions.

'$e \in \text{Prhn}$' for '$(Ee')(E\alpha)(Ee_1)...(Ee_k)(\langle e',\text{Prhd},e_1\rangle e \text{ v } \langle e',\text{Prhd},\alpha, e_1\rangle e \text{ v } ... \text{ v } \langle e',\text{Prhd},\alpha,e_1,...,e_k\rangle e)$'.

Clearly then

$(e)(e \in \text{Prhn} \supset e \in \text{AO})$,

$(e)e \in \text{AO}$.

It is useful to have a notation for differentiating between physical and conceptual prehensions. Let

'$e \in \text{PhysPrhn}$' abbreviate '$(Ee')(Ee_1)\langle e',\text{Prhd},e_1\rangle e$'

and

'$e \in \text{CncptlPrhn}$' abbreviate '$(Ee')(E\alpha)(Ee_1)...(Ee_k)(\langle e',\text{Prhd},\alpha,e_1\rangle e \text{ v } \langle e',\text{Prhd},\alpha,e_1,...,e_k\rangle e)$'.

Then

$(e)(e \in \text{Prhn} \equiv (e \in \text{PhysPrhn} \text{ v } e \in \text{CncptlPrhn}))$,

$(e)(e \in \text{PhysPrhn} \supset \sim e \in \text{CncptlPrhn})$,

$(e)(e \in \text{PhysPrhn} \supset e \in \text{Pos})$.

The inventory of the atomic sentential forms needed is not complete without ones for *ingression* and one for being *extensively connected with*. Let '$\alpha \text{ Ing } e$' express that α ingresses into e. Note that Ing, however, is not just the converse of the $\in$ for membership. '$\in$' is significant as between expressions for sets on both its left and right, as well as between expressions for actual occasions, eternal objects, and prehensions on the left and for sets on the right. 'Ing', on the other hand, is significant only with expressions for eternal objects on the left and expressions for actual occasions on the right. Similarly '$\alpha \text{ Ing } e_1,e_2$' expresses that the dyadic-relational eternal object α ingresses in e_1 and e_2 in that order. And so on, up to and including k, the degree of the primitive eternal-object constant of highest degree admitted. Clearly then

$(\alpha)(e)(\alpha$ Ing $e \supset e$ $^{+}$Prhd $\alpha,e)$,

$(\alpha)(e_1)(e_2)(\alpha$ Ing $e_1,e_2 \supset (e_1$ $^{+}$Prhd $\alpha,e_1,e_2 \cdot e_2$$^{+}$Prhd $\alpha,e_1,e_2))$,

and so on. (The converses need not hold.)

Let 'e EC e'' express that e is extensively connected with e'. Extensive connection is for Whitehead (p. 441) "the primary *relationship* of physical occasions. This ultimate relationship is *sui generis* and cannot be defined or explained. But its formal properties can be stated. ... Some general character of coordinate divisibility is probably an ultimate metaphysical character, persistent in every epoch of physical occasions. Thus some of the simpler characteristics of extensive connection ... are probably such ultimate metaphysical necessities." In accord with this surely 'EC' may be taken as a primitive and suitable principles governing it laid down axiomatically.

To summarize. The primitives needed thus far include 'Prhd' for prehending, variables for actual entities or occasions including prehensions, 'Neg' for negative ones, 'EO^1,' ... , 'EO^k' for sets of eternal objects, 'Ing' for ingression, and 'EC' for being extensively connected with. In addition, the standard underlying logic of truth-functions, quantifiers upon all kinds of variables admitted, and identity. Still further, a naive set theory is presupposed with variables upon sets of all manner of complexity. Finally, and most importantly, the resources of event logic are presupposed, particularly the theory of event-descriptive predicates.

5

CE(i) is provided here by the admission of the occasion or process variables 'e', and so on, as the only variables for entities in "the actual world." This latter is to be described wholly in terms of them. According to CE(vii) there are also fixed, immutable eternal objects, describable only in terms of their potentiality for [and of course actuality of] ingression into the "becoming" of actual entities. Eternal objects are values for special variables here with 'Ing' as a primitive. An eternal object α is a "pure potential" in the sense that, given any occasion e, α may bear Ing to e or may not. If it does, 'α Ing e' obtains, if it does not, '$\sim \alpha$ Ing e' does. 'α Ing e' thus expresses that the potentiality of α is "realized" in e. Of course eternal objects may also be described in terms of their potentiality for being prehended, and this is not excluded by CE(vii). CE(vii) gives in fact only a partial account of how eternal objects can be described.

According to CE (viii) "two descriptions are required for an actual entity," (a) one analytical of its "objectification in the becoming of other actual entities" (its "being"), and (b) one "analytical of the process which constitutes its own becoming" (its "becoming"). The objectification of an occasion e consists of just the actual entities that prehend it positively. Thus

'Objtn$e$' may abbreviate '$\hat{e}_1 e_2$ $^+$Prhd e'.[5]

This set is the *positive* objectification of e. The full objectification of e would include also entities that e negatively prehends. This is the *universe* of e. Thus

'Univ$e$' abbreviates '$\hat{e}_1 e_1$ Prhd e'.

The "description analytical of the becoming" of e seems to be the same as that required by CE(x), that "the first analysis of an actual entity, into its most concrete elements, discloses it to be a concrescence of prehensions, which have originated in its process of becoming." The notion of a concrescence is of course a key notion. We might attempt to get at it as follows. (Later, however, in §10, a better account will be given.)

To describe the becoming of e would be to disclose the *totality of its prehensions*. Thus

'Concr$e$' might abbreviate '$\hat{e}^1(Ee_1)...(Ee_k)(E\alpha)(\langle e, ^+Prhd, e_1\rangle e^1$ v $\langle e, ^+Prhd, \alpha, e_1\rangle e^1$ v ... v $\langle e, ^+Prhd, \alpha, e_1,...,e_k\rangle e^1)$'.

The concrescence of e, according to this definition, would be the set of all e's positive physical and conceptual prehensions. Negative prehensions would be excluded here on the grounds that, according to CE(xii), a "negative prehension holds its datum [what is prehended] as inoperative in the progressive concrescence of prehensions constituting the unity of the subject." To give this entire set, Concr$e$, would be to give a description analytical of the "becoming" of e. Thus would CE(viii)(b) and CE(x) be provided, if Concr$e$ is construed as a set of prehensions.

The *Principle of Process*, CE(ix), is to the effect that the "being" of e "is constituted by" its "becoming." The 'is constituted by' here need not perhaps be taken as the 'is' of identity nor the 'is' of predica-

---

[5] The use of the circumflex here is essentially that of *Principia Mathematica* for class- or set-abstraction.

tion, on this account of concrescence, but rather the 'is' of 'is constructed logically as'. How then may the Principle of Process be stated? Perhaps as follows.

$$(e)(e')(e'')((e'' \in \mathrm{Concr}^c e \cdot e' \in \mathrm{Objtn}^c e) \equiv \langle e, {}^+\mathrm{Prhd}, e' \rangle e'').$$

The disadvantage of this first account is that the concrescence of e is not an AO but a set of prehensions. This is awkward if it is thought that the 'is' of the Principle of Process should be taken more literally as sheer identity. The account to be given later, in which the concrescence of e is itself construed as an AO enables 'is' here so to be construed. For this, however, some notions of the calculus of individuals are needed.[6]

6

Some of the content of CE(xi) has been provided in § 4 above, in the notation for the distinction between physical and conceptual prehensions. The remainder is merely definitional. In particular, the subjective form of a prehension, "which is *how* that subject prehends that datum," must be accommodated. The *how* would presumably be described in an adverbial phrase. Where prehensions are regarded merely as occasions, the adverbial phrase may readily be accommodated by reference to a set.

Let μ be a class or set of prehensions determining a kind, so that '$e \in \mu$' expresses that e is a prehension of kind μ, in other words, that e has the subjective form μ. The content, of CE(xiii), that "there are many species of subjective forms, such as emotions, valuations, purposes, adversions, aversions, consciousness, etc.," may then be provided by admitting various primitive set constants in place of 'μ'. To say '$e \in \mathrm{Val}$', for example, would be to say that e is a *valuation*, '$e \in \mathrm{Emtn}$' that e is an emotion or emotive act, and so on. Let '$\mu \in \mathrm{SF}$' express primitively now that μ is a subjective form.

The *Principle of Relativity*, CE(iv), the "reformed subjectivist prin-

---

[6] See especially H. S. Leonard and N. Goodman, "The Calculus of Individuals and Its Uses," *The Journal of Symbolic logic* 5 (1940) : 45-55; N. Goodman, *The Structure of Appearance* (Harvard University Press, Cambridge : 1951), pp. 42 ff.; and J. H. Woodger, *The Axiomatic Method in Biology* (Cambridge University Press, Cambridge : 1937), Appendix E by A. Tarski. See also the author's *Pragmatics, Logic, and Linguistic Structure*, in preparation. The use of the notion of fusion would have been very useful for Whitehead and perhaps would have enabled him to dispense with the notion of a nexus.

ciple," is the principle that "it belongs to the nature of a 'being' [actual or eternal] that it is a potential for every 'becoming'," or "that every item in its universe is involved in each concrescence." The principle is a conjunction, one conjunct for the potentiality of occasions and k for that of EO^1's, EO^2's, and so on. Thus

$(e)((e')(e' \in \text{Univ'}e \supset e \text{ Prhd } e') \cdot (\alpha)(e')((\alpha \in EO^1 \cdot e' \in \text{Univ'}e) \supset e \text{ Prhd } \alpha,e') \cdot \ldots \cdot (\alpha)(e_1)\ldots(e_k)((\alpha \in EO^k \cdot e_1 \in \text{Univ'}e \cdot \ldots \cdot e_k \in \text{Univ'}e) \supset e \text{ Prhd } \alpha,e_1,\ldots,e_k))$.

Note that here and throughout there is nothing dangerous or suspect—the way in which the notions of modal logic are suspect—about Whitehead's use of 'potential' or 'potentiality'. The phrase 'pure potential' is merely a synonym for 'eternal object'. And to state that each occasion in the universe of e is a "potential" for the becoming of e is merely to state that e positively or negatively prehends each occasion in the universe of e. Some interpreters wish to read modal logic into Whitehead, but it is doubtful that this is needed. Whitehead seems to use 'potentiality' throughtout in the quite innocent way of a non-modal mathematician.

7

CE(v) is the principle that "no two actual entities originate from an identical universe." Thus

$(e)(e')(\text{Univ'}e = \text{Univ'}e' \supset e = e')$.

"The eternal objects are the same for all actual entities" in the sense of CE(iv), the Principle of Relativity. But they are not the same in the sense that they all ingress into the same occasion or occasions. Thus

$\sim (Ee)(\alpha)(\alpha \in EO^1 \supset \alpha \text{ Ing } e)$,

$\sim (Ee_1)(Ee_2)(\alpha)(\alpha \in EO^2 \supset \alpha \text{ Ing } e_1,e_2)$,

and so on.

"The nexus of actual entities in the universe correlate to a concrescence, is termed 'the actual world' correlate to that concrescence." Does Whitehead really wish to distinguish here the actual world of the concrescence of e from the universe of e? If so

'ActlWld'e' may abbreviate '$\hat{e}_1 e \,{}^+\text{Prhd } e_1$'.

The actual world of the concrescence of e consists of just the entities positively prehended, whereas the universe of e consists of all entities prehended either positively or negatively. These are, however, the same, all physical prehensions being positive.

According to CE(vi), "each entity in the universe of a given concrescence *can*, so far as its own nature is concerned, be implicated in that concrescence in one or other of many modes; but *in fact* it is implicated in only *one* mode; ... the particular mode of implication is only rendered fully determinate by that concrescence, though it is conditioned by the correlate universe, ..." Whitehead does not intend 'mode of implication' here to be a new technical phrase; presumably a mode of implication is merely the subjective form of a prehension. Accordingly CE(vi) might be construed as the folloiwng.

$(e)(e')(e_1)...(e_k)(\alpha)((\langle e, \text{Prhd}, e_1 \rangle e'$ ∨ $\langle e, \text{Prhd}, \alpha, e_1 \rangle e'$ ∨ ... ∨ $\langle e, \text{Prhd}, \alpha, e_1,...,e_k \rangle e') \supset (E\mu)(e' \in \mu \cdot \mu \in \text{SF} \cdot (\nu)((e' \in \nu \cdot \nu \in \text{SF}) \supset \nu = \mu)))$.

This principle asserts the existence and uniqueness of the subjective form of any prehension.

It is difficult to be clear as to the difference between "simple" and "complex" eternal objects. The easiest way is perhaps to consider those as simple whose proper names are taken as primitives of the system. Complex ones are then those introduced by definitions, in the definientia of which there is essential reference to more than one simple eternal object.

8

A nexus is, according to CE(xiv), "a set of actual entities in the unity of the relatedness constituted by their prehensions of each other, or—what is the same thing conversely expressed—constituted by their objectifications in each other." Presumably a set μ of AO's is then a nexus if it is non-null, and of any two members of it, one positively prehends the other. Thus

'$\mu \in$ Nex' may abbreviate '$(\sim \mu = \Lambda \cdot \mu \subset$ AO $\cdot (e)(e')((\sim e = e' \cdot e \in \mu \cdot e' \in \mu) \supset (e$ +Prhd e' ∨ e' +Prhd $e)))$'.

A proposition, CE(xv), is "the unity of certain actual entities in their potentiality for forming a nexus, with its potential relatedness partially defined by certain eternal objects which have the unity of one complex eternal object. The actual entities involved are termed the 'logical subjects', the complex eternal object is the 'predicate'." Recall that '$\alpha \in \text{EO}^n$' expresses that the eternal object α is an n-adic relation. α may be introduced by definition in terms of other eternal objects or perhaps itself be designated by a primitive relational constant. The notion of an n-adic proposition may then be introduced in terms of an ordered $(n + 1)$-tuple. Let

'$\mu \, \epsilon \, \text{Proptn}^{n}$' abbreviate '$(\text{E}e_1)...(\text{E}e_n)(\text{E}\alpha)(\text{E}\nu)(\mu = \langle \alpha, e_1,...,e_n \rangle \cdot \nu \, \epsilon \, \text{Nex} \cdot e_1 \, \epsilon \, \nu \cdot ... \cdot e_n \, \epsilon \, \nu \cdot \alpha \, \epsilon \, \text{EO}^n)$'.

A "proposition" here is of course nonlinguistic, although it may presumably be "represented" or "expressed" by a linguistic entity.[7]

CE(xvi) states that "a multiplicity consists of many entities, and its unity is constituted by the fact that all its constituent entities severally satisfy at least one condition which no other entity satisfies." A "condition" here may perhaps be construed as just a monadic eternal object. If so

'$\mu \, \epsilon \, \text{Mult}$' may abbreviate '$(\sim \mu = \Lambda \cdot (\text{E}\alpha)(\alpha \, \epsilon \, \text{EO}^1 \cdot (e)(e \, \epsilon \, \mu \equiv \alpha \, \text{Ing} \, e)))$'.

The eternal object α here of course need not be "simple" but can be of any desired complexity. Also the members of μ may be all manner of actual "entities," AO's or Prhn's, but not EO's or Proptn^n's.

What now is a "constrast" as required by CE(xvii)? Presumably any ordered couple of non-identical sets. Let

'$\mu \, \epsilon \, \text{Cntrst}$' abbreviate '$(\text{E}\nu)(\text{E}\nu')(\sim \nu = \nu' \cdot \mu = \langle \nu, \nu' \rangle)$'.

The diversity of ν and ν' here makes for some contrast. Here ν and ν' may be sets of all manner of entities, including EO's.

Nexūs, propositions, and multiplicities may also be prehended. The following definitions provide a notation for such "derivative" prehensions.

'$e \, \text{Prhd} \, \mu$' abbreviates '$(\mu \, \epsilon \, \text{Nex} \cdot (e_1)(e_1 \, \epsilon \, \mu \supset e \, \text{Prhd} \, e_1))$',

'$e \, \text{Prhd} \, \alpha, \mu$' abbreviates '$(\mu \, \epsilon \, \text{Nex} \cdot \alpha \, \epsilon \, \text{EO}_1 \cdot (e_1)(e_1 \, \epsilon \, \mu \supset e \, \text{Prhd} \, \alpha, e_1))$',

'$e \, \text{PrhdProptn}^n \, \mu$' abbreviates '$(\text{E}e_1)...(\text{E}e_n)(\text{E}\alpha)(\mu = \langle \alpha, e_1,...,e_n \rangle \cdot \mu \, \epsilon \, \text{Proptn}^n \cdot e \, \text{Prhd} \, \alpha, e_1,...,e_n)$',

'$e \, \text{PrhdMult} \, \mu$' abbreviates '$(\mu \, \epsilon \, \text{Mult} \cdot (e')(e' \, \epsilon \, \mu \supset e \, \text{Prhd} \, e'))$'.

The definienda read respectively 'e physically prehends the nexus μ', 'e conceptually prehends the $\text{EO}^1 \, \alpha$ as exemplified in the members of the nexus μ', 'e prehends the n-adic proposition μ', and 'e (physically) prehends the multiplicity μ'. The prehensions of contrasts seem less important, and need not be considered for the moment.

---

[7] For an important contribution to the metaphysical theory of propositions, see Frederic B. Fitch, "Propositions as the Only Realities," *American Philosophical Quarterly* 8 (1971) : 99-103. See also *Belief, Existence, and Meaning*, Chapters III and IX, and "On Fitch's Propositions and States of Affairs," in *Events, Reference, and Logical Form*.

Let 'e +Prhd μ', 'e -Prhd μ', 'e +Prhd α,μ', 'e -Prhd α,μ', and so on, be defined now in familiar fashion in terms of event logic. Thus
'e +Prhd μ' is short for '$(Ee')(\langle e,\text{Prhd},\mu\rangle e' \cdot e' \in \text{Pos})$',
and so on. Also let
'e PrhdProptn μ' abbreviate '$(e\,\text{PrhdProptn}^1\mu \vee ... \vee e\,\text{PrhdProptn}^k \mu)$'.

The following definition is also useful. Let
'e' PosPrhn e' abbreviate '$((Ee_1)\langle e,{}^+\text{Prhd},e_1\rangle e' \vee (Ee_1)(E\alpha)\langle e,{}^+\text{Prhd}, \alpha,e_1\rangle e' \vee ... \vee (Ee_1)...(Ee_k)(E\alpha)\langle e,{}^+\text{Prhd},\alpha,e_1,...,e_k\rangle e' \vee (E\mu)\langle e,{}^+\text{Prhd},\mu\rangle e' \vee (E\alpha)(E\mu)\langle e,{}^+\text{Prhd},\alpha,\mu\rangle e' \vee (E\mu)\langle e,{}^+\text{PrhdProptn},\mu\rangle e' \vee (E\mu)\langle e,{}^+\text{PrhdMult},\mu\rangle e')$',
and be read 'e' is a positive prehension by e'. Note that all manner of prehensions are included here, physical or conceptual, as well as those of nexūs, of propositions, and of multiplicities. Similarly 'e' NegPrhn e' may be defined, and then 'e' Prhn e' by disjunction.

In terms of all this, what now is the concrescence of e? The definition above could be changed to the following.
'Concr'e' abbreviates '$\hat{e}'e'$ PosPrhn e'.
This second account of concrescence would take into account e's prehensions of nexūs, of propositions, and of multiplicities, not explicitly accommodated in the previous definition. The inclusion of such is perhaps not essential, but it does no harm. Even here, however, the 'is' of the Principle of Process could not be construed as strict identity. The question thus still remains : how can 'Concr'e' be defined now so that the Principle of Process could be so stated?

Event logic presupposes the calculus of individuals, it will be recalled, and thus the notion of the *fusion* of a class or set of individuals, that is, the individual having as its parts all parts of the members of that class. Let
$$\text{'Fu'}\mu\text{'}$$
where μ is a set of AO's, be the fusion of μ. The concrescence of e may then be regarded as the fusion of the set of all e's positive prehensions. Thus
'Concr'e' may now abbreviate 'Fu'$\hat{e}'e'$ PosPrhn e'.

The Principle of Process, that the "being" of e "is" its "becoming," may now be stated with '$=$' in strict fashion as follows.
$(e)e = \text{Concr'}e$.
Also no two entities have the same concrescence and every entity has a unique one.

$(e)(e')(\text{Concr}'e = \text{Concr}'e' \supset e = e')$

and

$(e)(Ee')e' = \text{Concr}'e.$

Also of course

$(e)(Ee')(e' = \text{Concr}'e \cdot (e'')(e'' = \text{Concr}'e \supset e'' = e')),$

these last two principles being mere logical truths.

The "integration" of prehensions is handled here by means of the calculus of individuals. Given any two of e's prehensions, say e_1 and e_2, there is an "integrated" prehension, the logical sum of them, as it were, namely, $\text{Fu}'\{e_1,e_2\}$, i.e., the fusion of the set whose only members are e_1 and e_2. This seems a most reasonable and natural way of handling the integration of prehensions, and no doubt would have appealed to Whitehead had he known of the calculus of individuals.

9

The celebrated *Ontological Principle*, CE(xviii), states that "every condition to which the process of becoming conforms in any particular instance, has its reason *either* in the character of some actual entity in the actual world of that concrescence, *or* in the character of the subject which is in process of concrescence." Here it is difficult to know just how 'condition' is to be construed, perhaps as a set, perhaps as a monadic eternal object. The following two formulations suggest themselves.

$(\mu)(e)(e \in \mu \equiv ((Ee')(e' \in \text{ActlWld}'e \cdot e' \in \mu) \text{ v } (Ee_1)(E\alpha)(e \text{ Prhd } \alpha,e_1 \cdot e_1 \in \mu) \text{ v } \ldots \text{ v } (Ee_1) \ldots (Ee_k)(E\alpha)(e \text{ Prhd } \alpha,e_1,\ldots,e_k \cdot e_1 \in \mu \cdot \ldots \cdot e_k \in \mu))),$

$(\alpha)(e)(\alpha \in \text{EO}^1 \supset (\alpha \text{ Ing } e \equiv ((Ee')(e' \in \text{ActlWld}'e \cdot \alpha \text{ Ing } e') \text{ v } (Ee')(E\beta)(e \text{ Prhd } \beta,e' \cdot \alpha \text{ Ing } e') \text{ v } \ldots \text{ v } (Ee_1) \ldots (Ee_k)(E\beta)(e \text{ Prhd } \beta,e_1,\ldots,e_k \cdot \alpha \text{ Ing } e_1 \cdot \ldots \cdot \alpha \text{ Ing } e_k)))).$

The "character of the subject which is in process of concrescence" is here given in terms of the character of the entities prehended by the subject. Both the foregoing formulations seem legitimate ways of reading CE(xviii).

CE(xix) states that "the fundamental types of entities are actual entities, and eternal objects; and that the other types of entities only express how all entities of the two fundamental types are in community with each other in the actual world." In accord with this, special variables for AO's and for EO's have been introduced. No special variables for prehensions are needed, these being handled as a special kind of AO in terms of the primitive 'Prhd'. All other kinds of entities are derivative.

Ce(xx) seems to be merely definitional. To *function* "means to contribute determination [*definiteness* and *position*] in the nexus of some actual world." Definiteness is "the illustration of select eternal objects, and 'position' is relative status in a nexus of actual entities." Thus here one may say that an actual entity e gives the definiteness of eternal object α to e' if and only if e positively prehends α relative to e'. More generally,

'e Dfnts α,e'' abbreviates '$(e\ {}^+\text{Prhd}\ \alpha,e'\ \text{v} \ldots \text{v}\ (Ee_1)\ldots(Ee_k)(e\ {}^+\text{Prhd}\ \alpha,e_1,\ldots,e_k \cdot (e' = e_1\ \text{v} \ldots \text{v}\ e' = e_k)))$'.

One could add that e' is a member of a nexus here, but this seems hardly necessary. For the definition of 'position' or of 'giving position to', notions from the theory of extensive connection would be needed.

CE(xxi), on the other hand, combines a definition with a statement or principle. "An entity is actual, when it has significance for itself. By this it is meant that an actual entity functions in respect to its own determination. Thus an actual entity combines self-identity with self-diversity." According to this no doubt

$(e)(e\ \epsilon\ \text{AO} \equiv e = \text{Concr}'e)$,

so that e is an AO if and only if it is identical with its concrescence. Further, although of course

$(e)e = e$,

yet

$(e) \sim (Ee')(Ee'')(\langle e, \text{Prhd}, e''\rangle e' \cdot e = e')$,

so that self-identity combines with self-diversity, in the sense that no actual entity is (literally) identical with any one of its own prehensions.

CE(xxiii) is merely definitional of 'self-functioning', 'immediacy', or 'real internal constitution', in terms presumably of 'concrescence'. Thus

'RIC'e' is defined as 'Concr'e'.

More specifically, according to CE(xxiv), the "functioning of one actual entity in the self-creation of another actual entity is the 'objectification' of the former for the latter actual entity." Thus

'e' Func e' abbreviates '$e\ \epsilon\ \text{Objtn}'e'$'.

And the "functioning of an eternal object in the self-creation of an actual entity is the 'ingression' of the eternal object in the actual entity." Clearly, however, eternal objects also "function" in their role of being conceptually prehended. Thus

'α Func e' abbreviates '$(\alpha \text{ Ing } e \text{ v } (Ee')e \text{ Prhd } \alpha,e' \text{ v } \ldots \text{ v } (Ee_1)\ldots (Ee_k)e \text{ Prhd } \alpha,e_1,\ldots,e_k)$'.

10

Now let us consider the "phases" of a concrescence. Four are of especial interest, the originative phase, the creative phase, the satisfaction, and the objective immortality. The concrescence as a whole is the fusion of a set of prehensions, and these phases may be introduced in terms of fusions of suitable subsets of that total set.

The originative phase is the fusion of the set of just the positive physical prehensions of occasions in the antecedent world. Thus

'OrigPh'Concr'e' abbreviates 'Fu'$\hat{e}'(Ee'')\langle e,{}^{+}\text{Prhd},e''\rangle e''$'.

The objective immortality of e, on the other hand, is the fusion of the set of all the positive prehensions that are borne e by something or other. Thus

'ObjImmort'e' or 'ObjPh'Concr'e' abbreviates 'Fu'$\hat{e}'(Ee'')(\langle e'', {}^{+}\text{Prhd},e\rangle e'$ v $(E\alpha)\langle e'',{}^{+}\text{Prhd},\alpha,e\rangle e'$ v $\ldots$ v $(E\alpha)(Ee_1)\ldots(Ee_k)(\langle e'',{}^{+}\text{Prhd},\alpha,e_1,\ldots,e_k\rangle e'$ · $(e = e_1$ v $e = e_2$ v $\ldots$ v $e = e_k)))$'.

The objective immortality of e, or equivalently the objective phase of the concrescence of e, should be contrasted with the objectification of e, introduced in CE(viii). The former is the fusion of the relevant set of prehensions, the latter a set of AO's in general.

The creative phase and the satisfaction will be considered in a moment.

CE(xxvii) states that "in a process of concrescence, there is a succession of phases in which new prehensions arise by integration of prehensions in antecedent phases. In these integrations 'feelings' contribute their 'subjective forms' and their 'data' to the formation of novel integral prehensions; but 'negative prehensions' contribute only their 'subjective forms'. The process continues until all prehensions are components in the one determinate integral satisfaction." This CE combines a definition with a principle.

A phase of e in general is the fusion of a non-null subset of the set whose fusion is the concrescence of e. Thus

'$e' \in$ Ph'e' may abbreviate '$(E\mu)(E\nu)((e_1)(e_1 \in \nu \supset e_1 \text{ PosPrhn } e)$ · $e' = \text{Fu}'\mu$ · Concr'$e = \text{Fu}'\nu$ · $\mu \subset \nu$ · $\sim \mu = \Lambda)$'.

That there is a succession of phases resulting in a "new" prehension by integration of prehensions in "antecedent" phases, in which the subjective forms of the prehensions in the previous phases are "contributed" to the resulting "new" prehension, seems provided by the following principle.

$(e)(E\mu_1)(E\mu_2)(E\mu_3)(Fu'\mu_1 \; \epsilon \; Ph'e \; \cdot \; Fu'\mu_2 \; \epsilon \; Ph'e \; \cdot \; Fu'\mu_3 \; \epsilon \; Ph'e \; \cdot$
$(e_1)(e_2)(v_1)(v_2)((e_1 \; \epsilon \; \mu_1 \; \cdot \; e_2 \; \epsilon \; \mu_2 \; \cdot \; v_1 \; \epsilon \; SF \; \cdot \; e_1 \; \epsilon \; v_1 \; \cdot \; v_2 \; \epsilon \; SF \; \cdot \; e_2 \; \epsilon \; v_2)$
$\supset \; (Ee')(e' \; \epsilon \; \mu_3 \; \cdot \; e' \; \epsilon \; v_1 \; \cdot \; e' \; \epsilon \; v_2 \; \cdot \; e' \; PosPrhn \; e)))$.

Note that the "new" prehension e' will have the subjective forms of both e_1 and e_2. That the data of e_1 and e_2 are not "contributed" to e' where e_1 and e_2 are both negative, has already been noted in CE(xii).

11

The nine Categoreal Obligations seem merely to continue the list of CE's, with more emphasis on principles than on mere definitions.

The Category of Subjective Unity, CO(i), states that "the many feelings which belong to an incomplete phase in the process of an actual entity, though unintegrated by reason of the incompleteness of the phase, are compatible for integration by reason of the unity of their subject." By 'compatible for integration' here is meant merely having a common subjective aim.

Let 'Purps$_e$' designate primitively the set of e's prehensions that are *purposive*. Thus '$e' \; \epsilon \; Purps_e$' expresses that e' is one of e's purposes. Purposes are subjective forms, so that $Purps_e \; \epsilon \; SF$.

The notion of subjective aim was introduced in CE(xviii), but has not been introduced here in a technical way. "The 'subjective aim', which controls the becoming of a subject, is that subject feeling a proposition with the subjective form of purpose to realize it in that process of self-creation." Thus

'SA^n_e' may abbreviate '$\hat{e}'(e' \; \epsilon \; Purps_e. \; (E\alpha)(Ee_1)...(Ee_n)(E\mu)(\langle e,$
$^+Prhd,\alpha,e_1,...,e_n\rangle e' \; \cdot \; \mu \; \epsilon \; Proptn^n \; \cdot \; \mu \; = \; \langle\alpha,e_1,...,e_n\rangle)$'.

The n-adic subjective aim of e is the set of all e's purposes, so to speak, with which e prehends n-adic propositions. More generally,

'SA_e' may abbreviate '$\hat{e}'(e' \; \epsilon \; SA^1_e \; v \; e' \; \epsilon \; SA^2_e \; v \; ... \; v \; e' \; \epsilon \; SA^k_e)$'.

CO(i), the Category of Subjective Unity, now states that

$(e)(\mu)(e_1)(e_2)((Fu'\mu \; \epsilon \; Ph'e \; \cdot \; \sim Fu'\mu \; = \; Concr'e \; \cdot \; e_1 \; \epsilon \; \mu \; \cdot \; e_2 \; \epsilon \; \mu) \supset$
$(Ev)(v \; \epsilon \; SA_e \; \cdot \; e_1 \; \epsilon \; v \; \cdot \; e_2 \; \epsilon \; v))$.

An "incomplete phase" here is merely a phase that is not the whole concrescence.

Some prehensions are *decisional*, some not. Let 'Dcsn' designate the set of those that are. CO(ix), the Category of Freedom and Determination, "can be condensed into the formula, that in each concrescence whatever is determinable is determined, but that there is always a remainder for the decision of the subject-superject of that concrescence." In accord with this,

$$(e)(E\mu)(Concr^\epsilon e = Fu^\epsilon\mu \cdot (Ee')(e' \ \epsilon \ \mu \cdot e' \ \epsilon \ Dcsn) \cdot (Ee')(e' \ \epsilon \ \mu \cdot$$
$$\sim e' \ \epsilon \ Dcsn)).$$

What now is the creative phase of a concrescence? Perhaps just the decisional members of some μ where $Fu^\epsilon\mu = Concr^\epsilon e$. Thus

'$CrPh^\epsilon Concr^\epsilon e$' may abbreviate '$Fu^\epsilon\hat{e}'(E\mu)(Fu^\epsilon\mu = Concr^\epsilon e \cdot e' \ \epsilon$ Dcsn $\cdot e' \ \epsilon \ \mu)$'.

And what is the satisfaction? Just the fusion of the set of all of *e*'s positive prehensions that are in the originitive and the creative phases.

'$Sat^\epsilon e$' abbreviates '$Fu^\epsilon\hat{e}'(e' \ \epsilon \ OrigPh^\epsilon Concr^\epsilon e \ v \ e' \ \epsilon \ CrPh^\epsilon Concr^\epsilon e)$'.

12

The Category of Objective Identity, CO(ii), demands that "there can be no duplication of any element in the objective datum of the 'satisfaction' of an actual entity, so far as concerns the function of that element in the 'satisfaction'." What now is an "element in the objective datum"? Simply a member of μ where $Fu^\epsilon\mu = Sat^\epsilon e$. And what is an "element in the objective datum of the satisfaction"? Presumably any of *e*'s positive prehensions. That there can be no duplication of them so far as concerns their function in the satisfaction would require that any two such elements of the same prehensional structure, so to speak, are identical. Thus CO(ii) seems to state that

$$(e)(e')(\mu)(e_1)(e_2)((e_1 \ \epsilon \ \mu \cdot e_2 \ \epsilon \ \mu \cdot Fu^\epsilon\mu = Sat^\epsilon e \cdot ((\langle e,^+Prhd,e'\rangle e_1 \cdot$$
$$\langle e,^+Prhd,e'\rangle e_2) \ v \ (E\alpha)(Ee_3)...(Ee_{k+2})((\langle e,^+Prhd,\alpha,e_3\rangle e_1 \cdot \langle e,^+Prhd,$$
$$\alpha,e_3\rangle e_2) \ v \ ... \ v \ (\langle e,^+Prhd,\alpha,e_3,...,e_{k+2}\rangle e_1 \cdot \langle e,^+Prhd,\alpha,e_3,...,e_{k+2}\rangle e_2))))$$
$$\supset \ e_1 = e_2).$$

CO(iii), the Category of Objective Diversity, specifies that "there can be no 'coalescence' of diverse elements in the objective datum of an actual entity, so far as concerns the function of those elements in that satisfaction." Thus

$(e)(e')(e'')(\mu)(e_1)(e_2)((e' \in \mu \cdot e'' \in \mu \cdot \text{Fu}^\iota\mu = \text{Sat}^\iota e \cdot \sim e_1 = e_2 \cdot$
$((\langle e,^+\text{Prhd},e_1\rangle e' \cdot \langle e,^+ \text{Prhd},e_2\rangle e'') \vee (E\alpha)(Ee_3)...(Ee_{k+1})((\langle e,^+\text{Prhd},\alpha,$
$e_1\rangle e' \cdot \langle e,^+\text{Prhd},e_2\rangle e'') \vee (\langle e,^+\text{Prhd},\alpha,e_1,e_3\rangle e' \cdot \langle e,^+\text{Prhd},\alpha,e_2,e_3\rangle e'')$
$\vee (\langle e,^+\text{Prhd},\alpha,e_3,e_1\rangle e' \cdot \langle e,^+\text{Prhd},\alpha,e_3,e_2\rangle e'') \vee ... \vee (\langle e,^+\text{Prhd},\alpha,e_3,...,$
$e_{k+1},e_1\rangle e' \cdot \langle e,^+\text{Prhd},\alpha,e_3,...,e_{k+1},e_2\rangle e'')))) \supset \sim e' = e'').$

The Category of Conceptual Valuation, CO(iv), concerns conceptual "derivation" as well as valuation. It requires that "from each physical feeling there is the derivation of a purely conceptual feeling whose datum is the eternal object determinate of the definiteness of the actual entity, or of the nexus, physically felt." Thus

$(e)(e')(\alpha)((e + \text{Prhd } e' \cdot \alpha \text{ Ing } e') \supset (Ee'')(e'' \in \text{Val} \cdot \langle e,^+\text{Prhd},\alpha,$
$e'\rangle e''))$

and

$(e)(\mu)((e +\text{Prhd } \mu \cdot (e')(e' \in \mu \supset \alpha \text{ Ing } e')) \supset (Ee')(\langle e,^+\text{Prhd},\alpha,\mu\rangle e' \cdot$
$e' \in \text{Val})).$

13

According to CO(v), the Category of Conceptual Reversion, "there is a secondary origination of conceptual feelings with data which are partially identical with, and partially diverse from, the eternal objects forming the data in the first phase of the mental pole." Here too, two principles are involved, one for AO's and one for nexūs. Thus

$(e)(e')(\alpha)((e +\text{Prhd } e' \cdot \alpha \text{ Ing } e' \cdot e +\text{Prhd } \alpha,e') \supset (E\beta)(\sim \beta = \alpha \cdot$
$(Ee_2)(\alpha \text{ Ing } e_2 \cdot \beta \text{ Ing } e_2) . e +\text{Prhd } \beta,e'))$

and

$(e)(\mu)(\alpha)((e + \text{Prhd } \mu \cdot (e')(e' \in \mu \supset \alpha \text{ Ing } e') \cdot e +\text{Prhd } \alpha,\mu) \supset (E\beta)(\sim$
$\beta = \alpha \cdot (Ee'')(\alpha \text{ Ing } e'' \cdot \beta \text{ Ing } e'') \cdot e +\text{Prhd } \beta,\mu)).$

Partial identity and partial diversity of eternal objects are handled here in the obvious way in terms of their ingression. They are "partially identical" whith each other in the sense that they ingress into a common object, and "partially diverse" in the sense that they are not identical.

The Category of Transmutation, CO(vi), requires that "... the prehending subject may transmute the *datum* of ... [a derived] conceptual feeling into a characteristic of some *nexus* containing those prehended actual entities among its members, or of some part of that nexus." In other words,

$(Ee)(Ee')(E\alpha)(e \ ^+Prhd \ e' \cdot \alpha \ Ing \ e' \cdot e \ ^+Prhd \ \alpha,e' \cdot (E\mu)(E\nu)(\mu \ \epsilon$
$Nex \cdot \nu \subset \mu \cdot e' \ \epsilon \ \nu \cdot e \ ^+Prhd \ \alpha,\nu)).$

The Category of Subjective Harmony, CO(vii), states that the "valuations of conceptual feelings are mutually determined by the adaptation of those feelings to be contrasted elements congruent with the subjective aim," Recall that Val is the set of prehensions that are valuations. CO(vii) may then be stated as follows.

$(e)(e')((e' \ \epsilon \ Val \cdot (E\alpha)(Ee_1)...(Ee_n)\langle e,^+Prhd,\alpha,e_1,...,e_n\rangle e') \supset e'\epsilon$
$SA^n_e)$, for $1 \leq n \leq k$.

Given the subjective aim of e, e's valuations are members of it. They are "contrasted" in the sense that they are not all identical.

$(e) \sim (e')(e'')((e' \ \epsilon \ Val \cdot (E\alpha)(Ee_1)...(Ee_n)\langle e,^+Prhd,\alpha,e_1,...,e_n\rangle e' \cdot$
$e'' \ \epsilon \ Val \cdot (E\alpha)(Ee_1)...(Ee_n)\langle e,^+Prhd,\alpha,e_1,...,e_n\rangle e'') \supset e' = e''),$
for $1 \leq n \leq k$.

Thus far there has been no need to mention the *intensity* of a prehension. Prehensions have been regarded merely as positive or negative, and presumably positive prehensions have a higher degree of intensity for their subjects than negative ones. CO(viii), the Category of Subjective Intensity, can best be accommodated by explicitly introducing a numerical measure for intensity. Let 'Deg(i)' be now primitively such that '$e \ \epsilon \ Deg(i)$' expresses that e is a prehension of intensity i, where i is some real number in the interval 0 to 1. Then

$$\text{'}e \ Prhd^i \ e'\text{''}, \text{'}e \ Prhd^i \ \alpha,e'\text{''},$$

and so on, may be introduced by definition in familiar fashion. The admission of a numerical measure in this way seems a very natural step. It will enable us to accommodate CO(viii) as well as to account for Whitehead's frequent mention of "graded envisagement" of both AO's and EO^n's.

Positive prehensions are now those with sufficiently high degrees of intensity, negative prehensions with low degrees. Just how high or how low? The matter is left open. Positive perhaps with intensity $\geq 1/2$, negative with intensity $< 1/2$? Much would depend upon the principles governing intensity to be laid down.

CO(viii) states that "the subjective aim, whereby there is origination of conceptual feeling, is at intensity of feeling (1) in the immediate subject, and (2) in the *relevant* future." All intensity is in the immediate subject, so that (1) here is provided by the notation. What now is the *relevant* future? Presumably just the AO's conceptually prehended in accord with some (propositional) interest or purpose. And how high is intense? This would depend upon the subject e. Let 'Hne' express that n is high for e. Then CO(viii) seems to state that

$(i)(e)(\alpha)(e_1)...(e_n)((e \; {}^{+}\mathrm{Prhd}^i \; \alpha,e_1,...,e_n \; \cdot \; \langle \alpha,e_1,...,e_n \rangle \; \epsilon \; \mathrm{Proptn}^n) \supset$
Hie), for $1 \leqq n \leqq k$.

(Many passages suggest that a numerical measure be introduced also for *degree of ingression*. Eternal objects perhaps do not ingress *simpliciter* but only to such and such a degree. With a numerical measure of intensity for prehensions available, it would seem natural to introduce also a measure for ingression. Thus

$$\text{'}\alpha \; \mathrm{Ing}^i \; e_1,...,e_n\text{'}$$

may express that α ingresses into $e_1,...,e_n$ to degree i. This notion would then supplant 'Ing' above. Then presumably

$(\alpha)(e)(\alpha \; \epsilon \; \mathrm{EO}^1 \supset (Ei)\alpha \; \mathrm{Ing}^i \; e)$,

and so on. Also

$(\alpha)(e)(i)(\alpha \; \mathrm{Ing}^i \; e \supset e \; \mathrm{Prhd}^i \; \alpha,e)$,

and so on.)

What, finally, is the Category of the Ultimate? " 'Creativity', 'many,' 'one' are the ultimate notions involved in the meaning of the synonymous terms 'thing', 'being', 'entity'. These three notions complete the Category of the Ultimate and are presupposed in all the more special categories." Whitehead goes on to explain that 'one' "stands for the general idea underlying alike the indefinite article ..., the definite article ..., and the demonstratives 'this' or 'that', and the relatives 'which' or 'what' or 'how'." Much linguistic analysis would be needed to explicate this sentence. The kind of unity required may perhaps be viewed, more generally, as the kind of unity provided by the notions of logic taken all together, the unity of a logical system. This is provided here by the whole systematic framework. The "many" are provided by the AO's and the EO^n's. "Creativity" is provided by the concrescences, including of course decisional prehensions. It itself "connot be characterized, because all characters are more special than itself. But creativity is always found under conditions, and describ-ed as conditioned." The Category of the Ultimate may thus perhaps be construed as merely the triple

$\langle \mathrm{AO},(\mathrm{EO}_1 \cup \mathrm{EO}_2 \cup ... \cup \mathrm{EO}^k),\hat{e}^{\text{'}}(Ee)(E\mu)(e^{\text{'}} \; \epsilon \; \mu \; \cdot \; \mathrm{Concr}^\epsilon e \; = \; \mathrm{Fu}^\epsilon\mu) \rangle$,

or more simply as

$$\langle \mathrm{AO},\mathrm{EO},\mathrm{Prhn} \rangle.$$

The theory of extensive connection is developed in Part IV of *Process and Reality* in some mathematical detail. Hence only the bare bones of the theory need be mentioned here.

Recall that '*e* EC *e*'' expresses primitively that *e* is extensively con-nected with *e*'. In terms of this a number of definitions are given (pp. 450 ff.), all of which can presumably now be reconstructed here.

Given the relation EC with the definitions and assumptions in Part IV, together with an underlying set theory, it is not surprinsing that suitable geometric foundations for physical science (in particular theories of space and time, of spatio-temporal position, and so on), are forthcoming, and in a variety of ways. Whitehead's is not the only one, and many alternatives clamor for attention. Discussion of details here must be left for another occasion.

14

Whatever the defects of the foregoing account of Whitehead's categoreal scheme may turn out to be on further research and closer inspection, surely it must be admitted that some (hopefully useful) steps have been taken towards clarifying its logical structure. Much work yet remains, and many improvements will no doubt be in order. There are alternative approaches to be explored, the one suggested above being merely one. Enough has been shown, however, it would seem, to suggest that Whitehead's entire cosmological theory may be accommodated within a suitable logical framework—if not within this one, then within one somewhat similar.

Some readers may question the importance of exhibiting the logical format of a metaphysical or cosmological theory in such detail. Some readers may question whether such a format can be given at all. They are convinced in advance that something fundamental has been left out that can never be accommodated in a logical system. They say in effect : *Mathematica sunt, non leguntur*. On the other hand, there are philosophers and logicians whose attitude is rather : *Metaphysica sunt, non leguntur*. Frege, it will be recalled, berated both attitudes.[8] What is needed is an exact account of how the two are interrelated. "The solution I am asking for," Whitehead com-mented of another context, "is not a phrase, however brilliant, but a solid branch of science, constructed with slow patience, showing in detail how the correspondence is effected."[9]

---

[8] In the Introduction to the *Grundgesetze der Arithmetik*, I. (Jena : 1893), p. xii.
[9] *The Aim of Education and Other Essays* (The Macmillan Co., New York : 1929), p. 158.

The foregoing account of Whitehead's categoreal scheme is thus of interest on several grounds. In the first place, Whitehead himself would have welcomed it. On one occasion, in fact, in conversation with the present author, he commented to this effect, adding that he would have attempted such an account himself had he had the time, but that it was essential to make the intuitive sketch first in the few remaining years allotted him for philosophical writing.

Secondly, many readers are puzzled as to the exact character of the categoreal scheme. What are "categories" for Whitehead anyhow? Some of his statements are supposed to be definitions, Which ones? Are some supposed to lay down fundamental principles axiomatically? Which are supposed to be logical consequences of which? Are some in effect semantical rules or mere informal explanations? What is the logical structure of the language Whitehead used? What are its primitives? How are the eternal objects related to sets? What precisely are prehensions? How are they related to relations? What precisely is a concrescence? How are they related to actual occasions? And so on. Whitehead's manner of writing invites these questions and sensitive readers ask them. However, one must work very hard indeed to get even inadequate answers. In fact they cannot be answered, it would seem, except on the basis of the detailed exhibition of a full logical format. The foregoing is, of course, merely a first approximation. Some of these questions can be answered to some extent on its basis, but not all.

Especially important here is the treatment of prehensions. It has usually been supposed that prehensions are a kind of event, but no one seems to have explored how they may be handled on the basis of an exact logic.

Another merit of the foregoing logical reconstruction is that it makes Whitehead easier to understand. Whitehead's opaque style is a stumbling block to many and is often difficult if not impossible to follow. Logical systems, on the other hand, are easy to "read," provided of course one is familiar with modern logic and the methods of system building and logical analysis.

It is often lamented that Whitehead's system is so general as to lack content or relevance for specific philosophical problems. Whitehead's thought is thus sometimes regarded as a *cul-de-sac* and without interest for contemporary analytic philosophy. To be sure, most of Whitehead's statements are couched in terms of universal quantifiers and only a few of them contain specific constants for either an AO, an EO^n, or a Prhn. As soon as a constant is introduced, however, there remains the task of characterizing it explicity. To do so is not the function of metaphysics, it might be thought, but of the specific discipline to which the term belongs. Consider, for example, 'Val' for valuations, 'Dcsn' for decisions, and the like. To help characterize the latter, the theory of decision would be useful. To help characterize 'Val', much analytic philosophy concerned with 'valuable', 'good', and so on, is needed. Whitehead does not seek to provide specific analyses of these constants—this is the task of more special disciplines. He seeks only to characterize notions of vast generality, which can then be exemplified in specific instances. In the light of this, Whitehead's work is seen to be of interest for contemporary analytic philosophy, in particular, if we replace his quantifiers and variables by suitable constants and then seek to determine their behavior.

Whitehead, more clearly perhaps than any previous writer, grasped the great philosophic relevance of modern logic. "When in the distant future," he noted on one occasion, logic "has expanded, so as to examine patterns depending on connections other than those of space, quantity and number—when this expansion has occurred, I suggest that Symbolic Logic, that is to say, the symbolic examination of pattern with the use of ... variables, will become the foundation of aesthetics. From that stage it will proceed to conquer ethics and theology." [10] Whitehead failed to remark that somewhere along the way it would conquer metaphysics and cosmology as well.

The author is indebted to the host of able Whitehead scholars, whose writings have helped pave the way for this present account. In particular thanks are due Professors Frederic B. Fitch, Charles Hartshorne, (the late) Henry Leonard, and Victor Lowe for important suggestions garnered either in conversations or from their writings.

[10] *Essays in Science and Philosophy* (Rider, London : 1948), p. 99.

II

ON HARTSHORNE'S *CREATIVE SYNTHESIS AND PHILOSOPHIC METHOD*

"FORTIS ET CONSTANTIS EST NON PERTURBARI IN REBUS ASPERIS, NEC TUMULTANTEM DE GRADU DEJICI, UT DICITUR."

1

Professor Hartshorne's recent book [1] is without doubt one of the most serious and sustained works on so-called process philosophy since the publication of *Process and Reality* itself. It invites the reader to think out to the depths the foundations of this view without sparing difficulties along the way. Above all, the "method of convenient ignorance"—*scientia non habet inimicum nisi ignorantem*—is not his, for few contemporary metaphysicians have been so consistently concerned with the relevance to their subject of recent work in the empirical sciences, mathematics, and above all, logic, as he. And few if any have to equal degree combined this interest with unusual sensitiveness to and concern for aesthetic, ethical, social, humane, and religious values. A synoptic vision of a total philosophy is given in this book, with fascinating side views, as it were, leading out into almost all the areas of thought with which philosophers throughout the ages have been concerned.

The present paper will deal only with some aspects of this total view, in particular, with its logical underpinnings. In addition, along the wayside, various critical or constructive comments will be offered on specific points, especially as concerns philosophic method.

One of Hartshorne's "basic methodological convictions" is (p. xvii) that "logic is the backbone of philosophy," and this view he shares with many philosophic logicians, some idealist and empiricist metaphysicians, and certainly with Liebniz, Peirce, Russell, Carnap, and Whitehead — perhaps even, although less clearly so, with Quine and

---

[1] Charles Hartshorne, *Creative Synthesis and Philosophic Method* (SCM Press Ltd., London : 1970).

Goodman. Hartshorne contends that "nothing is quite clear logically unless it can be put mathematically." To "put it mathematically," however, does not always require that the devices of "working" mathematics be used, involving such entities say as real numbers, Hilbert spaces, topological groups, and the like. Rather, it could be contended, what is required is a specifically given non-logical vocabulary in terms of which what one wishes to say can be stated clearly. In addition, of course, the usual notions of (first-order) logic are needed. To "put it mathematically" might be construed as involving fundamental reference to classes, sets, and relations as real objects. But such reference is often not needed and would not well accord with Hartshorne's quasi-nominalism.

The sheer "technical proliferation of formal logic" (p. 54) presents a difficulty to metaphysicians, Hartshorne thinks. "To master it is half a life-work. Can metaphysicians afford to know but little of this development?" he asks rhetorically. In answer, it is suggested (p. 82) that "formal logic, including finite arithmetic, is the one mode of analyzing reasoning that can claim maximal clarity and rigour. Whatever help philosophers can get from its results they ought to take advantage of. It is true and important that there is room for dispute as to how far we have the formal logic we need. The ideal of extensionality has, I believe, sharply limited results so far."

This answer seems admirable as far as it goes. It is not clear, however, that philosophers have fully availed themselves of the formal logic we do have. Nor have they concerned themselves with more recent developments of immediate relevance. The ideal of extensionality, for example, is an admirable one not lightly to be given up. As a matter of fact, it has scarcely ever been put to the test. It has been disregarded in favor of easier ideals. When put to the test, it surely has not "sharply limited results" in any appreciable way. But extensionality can be preserved only by bringing into account *metalogical* notions. Metalanguages in one form or another should be explicitly taken into account by the metaphysician.

2

Hartshorne speaks (p. 54) of "the contention of most logicians that truth is in no way time-bound, in contrast to the neo-classical doctrine that the reality which makes statements true is protean, and partly

new each time we refer to it. ... To call factual truths timeless is at
best like calling a whole a part of itself, a convenient convention,
not an insight into the proper or non-degenerate meaning of 'factual
truth'." It has often been urged that 'true' is best taken in the sense
of modern semantic theory. That theory characterizes 'true' much as
arithmetic may be said to characterize the integers. And just as there
is no alternative to arithmetic, there is no acceptable alternative
to semantics. Some ways of construing 'true' require that any reference
to time be placed in the sentence to which 'true' is to be applied. Other
methods allow significance to 'true at time t' in the metalanguage.
It is not clear precisely what Hartshorne understands by the contention that "truth is in no way time-bound." In either of the ways of
handling 'true' mentioned, it would seem, adequate account of time
can be given.

Consider the following:

' 'Dover Wilson is a lover of Shakespeare in 1950' is true',
and

' 'Dover Wilson is a lover of Shakespeare' is true in 1950'.

These two are no doubt equivalent sentences in a metalanguage
containing time designators in the way required and on the basis
of suitable definitions of 'true' and 'true at time t'.

Note that there need be no conflict here with the contention that
reality is "protean." In a sense, of course, Dover Wilson is never the
same in any two consecutive moments of his life, and the referent of
'Dover Wilson' on one occasion of its utterence is not the same as
on another. Nor are any two utterances of 'Dover Wilson' ever the
same. They are similar enough for various linguistic purposes, to be
sure. Linguistic elements or inscriptions are after all also real items in
the cosmos and hence share the "protean" character of reality.

" 'Lover of Shakespeare' is a universal," it is noted (p. 58), "since
it can have an indefinite number of instances. But it could not have
had instances prior to the existence of Shakespeare." Ordinarily of
course a proper name is not introduced into a language prior to there
being a person so to be named. But note, on the other hand, that Russellian descriptions of not yet existing objects or persons are always
available in great numbers. Thus 'admirer of the President of the
United States in 1980' is a meaningful phrase and can reasonably
be regarded as standing for a universal, even an *eternal* universal.
Hartshorne apparently would wish to speak here of an *emergent*

universal. The advantage of speaking of eternal universals is that they
need not be dated. Emergent universals, on Hartshorne's view, would
apparently have to carry a date on their sleeve. Thus 'lover of Shakespeare' is emergent up to a certain date, but actual or eternal thereafter.
'Admirer of the President of the United States in 1980' is emergent
up to 1980, but actual or eternal thereafter. Of course, much more
needs to be said about emergence, but it is not clear that much more
need be said about its connection with time.

Hartshorne objects to the *eternality* of Whitehead's eternal objects,
especially of emergent ones. "I do not believe that a determinate
colour is something haunting reality from all eternity, as it were,
begging for instantiation, nor that God primordially envisages a
complete set of such qualities. At this point I am no Whiteheadian,"
he writes. This is not the occasion to consider Hartshorne's views
on universals in depth but only to suggest that the theory of *virtual*
classes and relations seems to be the one best in accord with them.[2]
Perhaps it is partly to this theory that Hartshorne refers when he
says that "the nominalistic argument has never been more forcefully
put than in this century ..." Virtual classes and relations have no
existence prior to their members or terms — in fact they have no
existence at all in the sense of being values for variables. They may
be regarded as having existence only with their members. They may
be regarded as coming into being and as passing out of being with
their members. And so on. In any case, it seems that much of Hartshorne's doctrine of universals could be made to accord with the virtual
theory.

3

Hartshorne enumerates (p. 82 ff.) some "rather simple, though
neglected, truths of [about (!)] formal logic as it now stands" that
seem to him "quite relevant to traditional philosophical problems."
These have to do roughly with relations, with modality, and with
the classification of possible solutions to problems. Hartshorne
follows Peirce and Whitehead, great masters certainly, in taking relations seriously. He accuses Russell, however, of having missed the
point that "there is some truth in the concept of internal relations."
There may well be, but Hartshorne seems not too clear as to just

---

[2] On virtual classes, see *Belief, Existence, and Meaning*, Chapter VI.

what internal relations are supposed to be. Dyadic relations are, according to him, either *internal* or *external* to their terms. If a relation is internal to its term, it is in some sense "constitutive" of it; and if external, not. Perhaps it may be said here that if 'a R b', where 'a' and 'b' are constants designating objects of the discourse at hand, is itself an analytic (or logically true) statement of the language — assuming for the moment that there might be such statements of this form — then and only then is R internal to a and to b. But this would not quite be Hartshorne's view. For him, a relation may be internal to one term, external to another. It is difficult to see how this mode of speaking may be accommodated in terms of notions of modal logic, however, to which Hartshorne is friendly. It would seem natural to think that for him the notion of an internal relation, or of a relation's being internal to a term, may be described in terms of a modal operator N for necessity. 'N' is significant only in contexts of the form 'N *p*' where in place of '*p*' a sentence or sentential function is inserted. Thus 'N a R b' would express that R is internal to both a and b. The 'N' here governs the whole of 'a R b', however, and cannot operate on 'a' or 'b' singly.

More specifically, Hartshorne writes that "formal logic has made it clear that thought turns upon relations, and that the relation of subject ... [to] predicate, or of a member of a class to a class, or of a class to another class, are far from being the only fundamental relations in which subjects enter. Rather the relation of a subject to other subjects, Rabc ... is the essential or general principle, of which 'S is P' is the special case in which the other subjects are vacuous. But then, if relations are predicates, since relation to S includes S, subjects include other subjects." This last sentence seems obscure. Relations are not literally *predicates*, for the latter are mere signs or linguistic entities, the former not. Also the phrase 'relation to S includes S' is not clear. And in any case, 'includes' here is not to mean the same as in 'subjects include other subjects'. In this latter, inclusion can perhaps be construed as the relation of part to whole between individuals.

"A man does not simply have the predicates : knowing, loving, hating, and so forth; he has the predicates : knowing *X*, *Y*, ..., loving *X* but hating *Y*, and so on. Either what is in the man is mere knowing, loving, hating, with the object of these states simply outside them, not constitutive of them or of the man at all, or what is in the man is knowing, loving, hating just the objects he does know, love, hate.

Is not the latter the right view? But then there is some truth in the concept of internal relations." What Hartshorne has in mind here, it seems, is not concerned with "internal" relations perhaps so much as with Whitehead's Principle of Process (CE(ix), *P. & R.*, pp. 34-35) to the effect that the "being" of an entity *is* its "becoming" or that the entity is itself identical with its own concrescence. (Recall I above.) Thus every one of an entity's prehensions is a "part" of that entity. A man's knowing person *X*, loving *Y*, hating *Z*, and so on, according to that Principle, are "in" the man, so to speak, and enter fundamentally into his "real internal constitution," his concrescence. These reflections seem to provide in part what Hartshorne wishes to say here, and may all be accommodated without reference to the obscure notion of internal relation.

4

Hartshorne thinks that modal logic is needed in metaphysics, in particular, the principle that

$$N (p \cdot q) \equiv (N p \cdot N q),$$

where in place of '*p*' and '*q*' we put in sentences or sentential functions. This principle is supposed to show that "the necessary cannot include the contingent, and that the total truth, assuming there are both contingent and necessary truths, must be contingent." The analogous principle holds for analytic (or logical) truth also, handled metalinguistically. The total set of truths, according to the semantic account, includes both analytic and factual ones. The total set is "necessary" or "contingent" then, by definition, depending, respectively, upon whether all members are analytic or some factual. Hence the total set is "contingent." Thus whatever metaphysical use Hartshorne wishes to make of this modal principle can be achieved also in the metalinguistic formulation.

Hartshorne seems to think, however, that the metalogical handling of modality suggested will somehow not do. "It is important to realize that there is another theory of modality," he writes (p. 133). "This is the theory (a) that possibility and necessity are in the first place ontological (and only derivatively logical or linguistic) and (b) that they are ontological as *modi* of time or process. That is necessarily which is always; that happens of necessity which never fails to happen; that exists or happens contingently which exists or happens only at, during, or after, a particular or limited time." A theory that handles modality in accord with (b) would also accord with (a), so that only (b) need be considered here. Presumably the whole content of (b) can be accommodated with the help of universal quantifiers over times or events and with a suitable theory of temporal flow. That is necessary, then, that holds for all times, or holds of all events; that is contingent that holds only for some times or events. It is not clear that there is anything intrinsically modal here, however, but merely Whitehead's doctrine of "necessity in universality." Of course the theory of time or events needed and of temporal flow, must be spelled out, whether the treatment is in any real sense modal or not. (More will be said concerning this in a moment.)

The third item concerning the role of formal logic in metaphysics that Hartshorne calls attention to is a kind of method of exhaustion. "A basic precedure (pp. 84-5) in all thinking is to *exhaust possible solutions* to a problem and arrive at the best or truest by an elimination of those that are unsatisfactory. ... To be sure that one has exhausted possibilities, one must formalize the concepts." Surely, and to formalize is in part to enunciate a suitable non-logical vocabulary concerning the metaphysical subject matter at hand. "For example, it is fallacious to say that either God is finite or he is not finite. The real disjunction is, God is in all aspects finite, in no aspects finite, or in some aspects finite and in others not." To formalize this latter, the locution 'God is finite in aspect α' is presumably needed, with 'α' introduced as a variable ranging over aspects. "If a severely extensional logic cannot recognize aspects, then so much the worse for thus limiting logic. There can be a logic of aspects." Yes, an *applied* logic of aspects, the underlying basic logic being the usual extensional one. The admission of the locution 'God is finite in aspect α' need not occasion a change in the underlying logic. Rather, suitable axioms governing this new locution are to be laid down, these axioms providing the "logic" or theory of aspects. It is not clear at any point, however, that the "severely extensional" approach must break down. It may be, of course, that for an adequate rendition of the notion of aspect here, some metalinguistic notions of intensional semantics would be needed.

5

Talk of events leads immediately to the subject of event logic and an event ontology. Hartshorne's Chapter IX, "Events, Individuals and Predication : A Defense of Event Pluralism," contains both an argument for and a defense of the view "that the most analytically complete way of speaking is event-speaking, not thing- or substance-speaking." Not that the latter is given no place; the contention is rather that it is merely a "simplification or shorthand," eminently useful for many purposes. Event talk is metaphysically the more fundamental, however. A thoroughgoing event talk involves an ontology of events and events only. Enduring physical objects are construed then as sequences (or sums) of events related by genidentity, as Hartshorne notes.

The various arguments on behalf of event pluralism need not be reviewed here. It is not clear that they either singly or jointly constitute a "knockout blow," in Arthur Prior's phrase, against a substance-oriented metaphysics. Metaphysical views die hard, and improved formulations can render them well-nigh invulnerable. In any case, before process philosophy can be adequately assessed, the full event logic underlying it must be properly formulated. And similarly for the opposing view; no logically sound and fully developed theory of change or process seems to have been formulated on the basis of a substance metaphysics. To be sure, there are insights and suggestions. The suggestion that a full analysis of such notions as 'while', 'during', 'before', 'after', and so on, handled as sentential connectives is intriguing. But this seems not to have been worked out in detail. And even if it were, it is not clear that such a theory would achieve all that would be wished or hoped of it.

6

Many metaphysicians take a rather cavalier attitude to logic, modern syntax, sematics, and the like. There is a vast multiplicity of logics, it is thought, so why should some one be used rather than another? — it is asked. Also logic is hard work and it is often difficult to make it do just what the metaphysician wants. It never seems quite to fit; therefore, let us disregard it altogether — is the attitude. Also it is very easy to make errors in logico-metaphysical matters.

Even the greatest logicians, both philosophic and mathematical ones, are not above reproach in this regard.

A moment's reflection should be sufficient to see that none of these 'arguments," if such they be, carries much weight. Convenient ignorance is a method much condemned in the sciences and the humanistic disciplines, as Hartshorne agrees, and no doubt should be in philosophy also. The argument from multiplicity fares no better. There are alternative physical theories, but we do not therewith justifiably reject physics. And strong reasons can be put forward in favor of regarding the standard, classical, first-order logic as the fundamental one.

The hard-work argument likewise carries little weight. Why philosophy should have become easy in our time — easier than ever before in its history, as Russell has remarked of the Oxford way of doing it—and the sciences and other humanistic disciplines increasingly difficult, is by no means clear. That the fit is never quite perfect is surely no reason for not always going on to try to get the more exact measure. Finally, concerning essentially the argument from error, Popper has urged forcefully that "error elimination" is an essential step often in the advance of objective knowledge.[3] Why errors should be allowed in mathematics, science, and the humanities generally, merely as items to be corrected, but regarded as fatal to the use of logical methods in philosophy is a mystery fathomable only by the sociologist of knowledge.

Coupled with the metaphysician's frequent disregard of logic is a *principle of premature rejection*. The riches of standard, classical logic sometimes become apparent only after much careful thought. Much of the widespread cultivation of kinds of logic alternative to the classical one is seen to be unnecessary if the latter (with extensions) is really pressed for its nectar.

Hartshorne contends (p. 69) that "metaphysical statements are not opposed to anything except wrong ways of talking. Metaphysical error is exclusively a matter of confusion, inconsistency, or lack of definite meaning, rather than of factual mistakes." Also (p. 158), "the widespread view that there is no genuine logic of metaphysical conceptions, no rules of the game of talking metaphysically, seems to me incorrect. ... Metaphysical truths are necessary, not factual."

---

[3] See especially K. R. Popper, *The Logic of Scientific Discovery* (Hutchinson, London : 1959) and *Conjectures and Refutations* (Routledge and Kegan Paul, London : 1963).

These contentions are central to Hartshorne's conception of deity and to his discussion of the "theistic" proofs and the ontological argument. To assess them one must of course have a very clear view as to just how metaphysics presupposes logic. We shall return to this topic in a moment.

7

Fundamental to Hartshorne's philosophical view also is the contention that 'Something exists' is a necessary truth. This seems essential to his view as perhaps no other single contention. It is precisely *Russell's* logic, however, which Hartshorne seems to condemn throughout, that condones such a statement as necessary. Thus, where 'Q' is any one-place predicate, the much-discussed formula
$$'(Ex)(Qx \lor \sim Qx)'$$
states that there is at least one object. Further, this statement is a logical or analytic truth, and thus presumably "necessary" in one reasonable meaning of that word. Let us not prematurely reject this principle by thinking that it cannot be made to provide, in part at least, what Hartshorne needs.

So far, so good. 'Something exists' becomes analytic, if we let, as is frequently done,

'E!x' abbreviate '$(Qx \lor \sim Qx)$'.

Then 'E!' in effect functions as a predicate for existence. Hartshorne wishes to show also that 'God exists' is a necessary truth.

Although Hartshorne claims not to be a Whiteheadiean in this or that regard, surely he is a Whiteheadian in many regards. Let us, for present purposes anyhow, suppose that Hartshorne distinguishes as Whitehead does the primordial and consequent natures of God. These two "natures" must be handled rather separately and of course allowed to have very different properties. It might be that God on his consequent side is a "necessary" being but on his primordial side a "contingent" one. Indeed, this seems to be Hartshorne's view, although *prima facie* one might have supposed the matter the other way around, the primordial nature as necessary, the consequent one contingent. For Whitehead, the matter is unimportant; for Hartshorne it is crucial. It is not "necessary" for him that God primordially envisages a complete set of eternal objects. It is, however, necessary for God to exist. We must thus look for a way of accommodating the consequent nature as a necessary being and the primordial one as contingent, in accord with Hartshorne's view.

Let now

'*cng*' abbreviate 'Fu'$\hat{e}e = e$',

where again the notion of fusion from the calculus of individuals is used. The consequent nature of God, *cng*, in the fullness of all cosmic time, so to speak, is the fusion of the class of all events, states, acts, processes, and so on. This is the consequent nature of God viewed timelessly. If God is viewed relative to a given time, another definition is needed. Strictly, in event logic, times are mere logical constructs and we have no right to speak of them as yet. Instead, let us speak loosely of the time of the event or state e as the time during which e takes place or happens. Let 'e_1 Up e_2' express that the time of e_1 is wholly before that of e_2 or includes it but does not extend beyond it into the future. In loose words, the time of e_1 is *up to* that of e_2. (There are, of course, difficulties with this notion in connection with special and general relativity, as Hartshorne in effect notes (pp. 123 ff.), that would have to be faced in a fuller account.) The consequent nature of God up to the time of e may then be introduced as follows.

'*cng^e*' abbreviates 'Fu'$\hat{e}'e'$ Up e'.

cng^e is merely the fusion of all events up to e.

Let 'E!e' be defined as above, with the event variable in place of 'x'. The only "things" we now have, in accord with event pluralism, are events, states, and the like. 'Something exists' becomes then presumably

$$(Ee)E!e,$$

with 'E!' as the predicate for existence. This statement is analytic if the usual classical logic of quantifiers is presupposed for the event variables. But of course

$$(e)E!e,$$

'Everything exists', also becomes analytic. Hartshorne wishes to assign necessary existence only to God, however, but not to all his creatures. This may perhaps be accomplished as follows.

Necessary existence is somehow *all-inclusive*. There is one and only one such entity and it contains all events as parts. The one necessary being is such that there is no greater, or more inclusive, entity. Perhaps it is even that than which no greater can be conceived — although for this contention the logic of 'conceives' would have to be explored. (See VIII below.) Let 'e_1 P e_2' express that e_1 is a part of e_2 in the sense essentially of the calculus of individuals, and 'e_1 B e_2', that e_1 is wholly before e_2 in time. Then, in accord with Hartshorne's view,

'N!e' may abbreviate '(E!e · (e')e' P e)'.

(The clause 'E!e' in the definiens here may be dropped in view of the analyticity of '$e = e$'.) Similarly

'N!$e^{e''}$' may abbreviate '(E!e · (e'')(e'' Up e' ⊃ (e'' P e · ~ (Ee'')(e' B e'' · e'' P e)))'.

The definienda here reads respectively, 'e exists necessarily' and 'e up to e' exists necessarily'.

We then have analytic existence and uniqueness principles as follows.

(Ee)N!e,

(e_1)(e_2)((N!e_1 · N!e_2) ⊃ $e_1 = e_2$),

(e)(Ee')N!e'^e,

(e)(e_1)(e_2)((N!$e_1{}^e$ · N!$e_2{}^e$) ⊃ $e_1 = e_2$),

as well, of course, as

(e)(N!e ≡ $e = cng$),

N!cng,

and

(e)N!cng^e.

There is at least one necessary, all-inclusive being. There is at most one necessary, all-inclusive being. Given any e, there is at least one necessary being up to e. Given any e, there is at most one necessary being up to e. Given any e, it is a necessary, all-inclusive being if and only if it is identical with the consequent nature of God. The consequent nature of God exists necessarily as an all-inclusive being. And given any e, the consequent nature of God up to e exists necessarily.

8

The primordial nature of God, *png*, may be introduced in terms of conceptual valuations, as with Whitehead. Let 'e_1 Prhd α, e_2' express that e_1 prehends the eternal object α relative to e_2, as in I above. For Whitehead the *png* may be regarded as the fusion of all conceptual prehensions that are valuations. Let '$e \in$ Val' express, also as in I, that e is a valuational act or state and let k be the degree of the primitive eternal-object constant of highest degree admitted. Finally, also as in I, let formulae such as '⟨e_1,Prhd,α,e_2⟩e' express that e is a conceptual prehension, i.e., an event or state of e_1's prehending α with respect to e_2. Then '*png*' may abbreviate 'Fu'$\hat{e}$(Eα)(Ee_1)...(Ee_k)((($\langle cng$,Prhd,$\alpha,e_1\rangle e$ v ... v $\langle cng$,Prhd,$\alpha,e_1,...,e_k\rangle e$) $\cdot$ e ϵ Val)'.

The primordial nature of God is thus the fusion of the class all the consequent nature's conceptual prehensions that are valuations.

For Hartshorne this definition will not do, for *png* contains, in accord with it, all *cng*'s valuational acts or states, past, present, and future. For him, only valuational *e*'s *up to* a given *e'* should be admitted. For him, presumably the e_1, ... , e_k here also should be restricted in this way. Thus, for him, we may perhaps let

'*png*$^{e'}$' abbreviate 'Fu'$\hat{e}$(Eα)(Ee_1)...(Ee_k)((($\langle cng$,Prhd,$\alpha,e_1\rangle e$ v ... v $\langle cng$,Prhd,$\alpha,e_1,...,e_k\rangle e$) $\cdot$ e_1 Up e' $\cdot$ ... $\cdot$ e_k Up e' $\cdot$ e Up e' $\cdot$ e ϵ Val)'.

Clearly now

E!*png*,

(*e*)E!*png*^{e},

(*e*)*png*^{e} P *png*,

png P *cng*,

and

(*e*)*png*^{e} P *cng*^{e}.

The primordial natures exist and are parts of the respective consequent natures, because every conceptual valuation is after all a prehension or event or state. And clearly every *png*^{e} is a part of the full *png*, this latter being the most inclusive possible.

Note that the underlying logic for the above is provided by axioms and rules for first-order logic including identity, axioms for the calculus of individuals, for the spatio-temporal topology, and principles of existence governing the event-descriptive predicates, as in event logic. In addition, general principles concerning prehensions, such as perhaps those of Whitehead's categoreal scheme, are included, although these are an addendum and not a part of event logic. The analytic truths of the entire system then comprise just those provided in this way.

Note that *png* and all *png*^{e}, lack *necessary* existence.

$\sim$ N!*png*

and

(*e*) $\sim$ N!*png*^{e}.

They lack the fullness or universality required for necessity. On the other hand, the statements that they exist are themselves analytic or necessary statements. We must distinguish between necessary truth and necessary being, a distinction Hartshorne does not seem to make.

Necessary being involves fullness or all-inclusiveness, so to speak, as well as analyticity, necessary truth analyticity only.

9

A further comment concerning fullness. Note that the necessary being *cng* really is the fullest or most inclusive possible, containing all events, states, acts, processes, happenings, both mental and physical, all sign-events including all truths, all syntax, all semantics, all utterances, all acceptances, all beliefs, all that is known or "conceivable," all objects of Poppers' "third world" of objective spirit, all religious acts, all acts of devotion, of love, of gentleness, of hope, of charity, all valuations, all things of beauty and excellence, the beautiful, the good. This is indeed a true fullness, than which there is no greater, and perhaps than which no greater can be conceived.

Note that *cng* is not just the physical universe. "You might think (pp. 235-236) that reality as a whole, or the universe, could ... be put in the place of God. But then in what sense is reality a whole, or in what sense is the universe an individual? ... God is unsurpassably inclusive and also unsurpassably integrated or unified. IIe is thc all as an individual being." Here *cng* is an event in the sense of being a value for the variables 'e' and so on. *cng* is "unsurpassably integrated or unified" in being the fusion of all there is or can be in heaven or earth. Moreover, *cng* is an individual being in the same sense that events, states, creatures, and so on, are.

It was suggested above that perhaps *cng* can be regarded as that being than which no greater can be conceived. If concepts are relativized to the language at hand, conceivability can be handled in terms of expressibility in language. One and the same entity may be conceivable, including perhaps a null entity, then, under various linguistic descriptions, each of which presumably should be such as in no way to involve a contradiction. Thus 'golden mountain and not golden' would not be suitable as a linguistic description of anything. *cng* then contains all "consistently thinkable" entities — C.I. Lewis' phrase — including of course the null individual under various descriptions.

Note also that the treatment of the necessary being here, as distinguished from necessary truth, is, as Hartshorne wishes it to be, "in the first place ontological" and in a suitable sense depends upon "time or process." The predicate 'N!' is a predicate defined within the object language and a universal quantifier over the e's is needed in the definiens. Further, "that is necessarily which is always; that happens of necessity which never fails to happen ..." If N!e, then of course e "is always," for all e. To make the phrase 'is always' precise, a universal quantifier over times would be required, but in any case the foregoing statement would presumably obtain. Similarly if 'fails to happen' were made suitably precise, it would obtain that if N!e then there is no time at which e fails to happen, for all e.

There is one and only necessary being with the fullness required. Clearly, however, there is no necessary golden mountain, for not all e's would be parts of it. The foregoing considerations thus bear some semblance to the Anselmian argument. (Again, see VIII below.)

Note that 'cng' and 'cng^e' in the foregoing may be regarded as nominalistic notions. They are defined without reference to "abstract objects," sets, relations, or "eternal objects" as values for variables. (The sets used in the definientia may be regarded as virtual.) On the other hand, 'png' and 'png^e' are not handled nominalistically. The presence of the quantifier '$(E\alpha)$' in the definientia is essential. Can we reconcile this circumstance with Hartshorne's purported nominalism? As already suggested, Hartshorne perhaps may not accept png but only the png^e's. But it is not clear that he really needs the png^e's either. The matter may be left open. Perhaps he is a kind of quasi-nominalist, somewhat like Quine. The only notions that truly please either are nominalistic ones, but here and there, in the theory of deity or in mathematical set theory, non-nominalistic notions are to be admitted grudgingly *faute de mieux*.

Finally, note that the notion 'cng' comes out rather well with respect to Hartshorne's desiderata (pp. 264-265) of "contrast," "contingent concreteness," "divine freedom," "divine inclusiveness," and the "classical" principle, perhaps with '$+$' on all counts.

Little has been said here concerning freedom and creativity. These are provided in the Whiteheadian theory of prehensions and it is not clear that Hartshorne parts from that account in key respects.

It might legitimately be objected that much has been left out of the "rational reconstruction" here of some aspects of Hartshorne's views. Indeed, the account is by no means a final one and no doubt much can be improved upon. A kind of logical "backbone" has been provided, however, which goes a certain distance surely in helping to explicate some of Hartshorne's views, or at least some views rather close to his.

Hartshorne himself laments (p. 97) that he has not cultivated formal logic more than he has, in particular in connection with metaphysics. On this point he offers the old injunction "Do as I say, not as I do." In trying to do as he says in this paper, we have merely tried to help him do on a firmer logical basis some of the things he has tried to do. If the treatment is not wholly satisfactory, this should not be taken as a fatal objection. Let us then merely try to do better. "Logic (p. 260) [in the broad sense here] has a future as well as a past and present," as indeed does metaphysics!

III

ON THE WHITEHEADIAN GOD

"Deo dignus vindici nodus."

1

It is significant that Whitehead makes no explicit reference to God in the preliminary delineation (pp. 27-45) of the categoreal scheme in *Process and Reality*. This is no accident, for Whitehead's God emerges only as a construct in terms of the metaphysically basic entities, namely, actual occasions, eternal objects, and prehensions, prehensions in turn being themselves a kind of actual occasion. Immediately, however, amends are made in the following chapter, "Some Derivative Notions." We are straitaway told that the "primordial created fact is the unconditional conceptual valuation of the entire multiplicity of eternal objects. This is the 'primordial nature' of God. ... God is the primordial creature; but the description of his nature is not exhausted by this conceptual side of it. His 'consequent nature' results from his physical prehensions of the derivative actual entities ..."

That the notion of God is handled as derivative does not mean of course that it is in any way less fundamental or unimportant than the non-derivative ones. For Whitehead, "God [p. 521] is not to be treated as an exception to all metaphysical principles, invoked to save their collapse," as in some of the great historical systems. "He is," rather, "their chief exemplification." The entire system, in fact, may be viewed as providing "a certain rendering of the facts" concerning God's nature. "There is nothing ... in the nature of proof," in the sense of any of the traditional proofs for God's existence, and the system is supposed to stand or fall pretty much as a whole. In adding another speaker to Hume's *Dialogues Concerning Natural Religion*, as he says he does (p. 521), Whitehead is inviting us to dwell "upon the tender elements of the world, which slowly and in quietness operate by love."

He wishes to elucidate "somewhat exceptional elements in our conscious experience — those elements which may roughly be classed together as religious and moral intuitions." The extraordinary appeal of Whitehead's approach is that it seeks to accommodate these exceptional elements in the same categoreal framework that it seeks to accommodate logic, mathematics, and empirical science, and not just superficially in a telling phrase or two, but with a reasonably full delineation of basic notions, definitions, and fundamental principles.

Here, as in I above, there is no question of merely keeping to the letter of what Whitehead has written. It is the spirit that guides us, even if the result should seem somewhat remote from the text. Thus it is perhaps not literally Whitehead's view that is discussed here, but merely an approximation to it.

2

The consequent nature of God, *cng*, was introduced in the preceding paper as the fusion of the class of all AO's so that

'*cng*' abbreviates 'Fu'$\hat{e}e = e$'.

The *cng* thus comprises, in its total cosmic fullness, all occasions, all sums of them [nexūs], all prehensions both physical and conceptual, and thus all valuations, adversions, aversions, hopes, fears, loves, hates, and so on.

The primordial nature, on the other hand, was regarded as the fusion of the class of the conceptual valuations of the *cng* with respect to all EO's relative of course to all AO's. Thus

'*png*' was taken to abbreviate 'Fu'$\hat{e}(E\alpha)(Ee_1)...(Ee_k)((\langle cng,\text{Prhd}, \alpha,e_1\rangle e \ v \ ... \ v \ \langle cng,\text{Prhd},\alpha,e_1,...,e_k\rangle e) \cdot e \ \epsilon \ \text{Val})$'.

The *png* is, according to this definition, the fusion of *all* of the *cng*'s conceptual prehensions that are valuations and with respect to all EO's.

This definition is not quite adequate, however, it seems, for it does not take into account the numerical degrees of the valuations. The valuation is complete, of course, in the sense that every EO is valuated with respect to all AO's. "By reason of this complete valuation," Whitehead writes (p. 46), "the objectification of God in each derivate actual entity, results in a graduation of the relevance of eternal objects to the concrescent phases of that derivate occasion." The "graduation" here, it seems, can best be provided by a numerical measure. Thus, in place of the preceding definition, the following is suggested.

'*png*' may abbreviate 'Fu'$\hat{e}$(Ei)(Eα)(Ee_1)...(Ee_k)(($\langle cng,$Prhd$^i,\alpha,e_1\rangle e$
v ... v $\langle cng,$Prhd$^i,\alpha,e_1,...,e_k\rangle e$) · $e \, \epsilon$ Val · $0 \leq i \leq 1$)'.
Here each EO is valued to just such and such a degree with respect to its "relevance" to each AO.

In the definientia of these two definitions of '*png*', it should be noted, it is the *cng* as a whole whose valuations determine the "relevance" or order of all eternal objects. However, Whitehead nowhere stipulates this nor does he anywhere say just *whose* primordial valuations constitute the primordial nature. This seems an important omission. The valuations cannot be those of any AO, for all such valuations would be "conditioned" by the world antecedent to that AO. There thus seems to be in Whitehead's cosmos nothing to perform the primordial valuations other than *cng* as a whole. These valuations would then seem to be "conditioned," however, for *cng* is merely the cosmos as a whole. The *cng*'s conditioned valuations should be distinguished from its unconditioned ones. Also it might be thought that *cng*'s valuations are given only *after* all creation, not *with* it, as Whitehead insists (p. 521). Their "relevance" could thus never be operative in actuality. A way out of these difficulties, if such they are, suggests itself as follows.

Consider again a form of the kind
$$'\langle e_1,\text{Prhd},e_2\rangle e'.$$
Ordinarily where an instance of such a form holds, e is one of the prehensions constituting e_1's "real internal constitution," in which case e bears P to e_1. Ordinarily a prehension e must have a "subject" e_1 *distinct* from itself and distinct from its "object" or "datum" e_2. Clearly the subject e_1 must always be distinct from the datum e_2 and the prehension e must also always be distinct from the datum. The question arises, however, as to whether a prehension could ever be *its own subject*. In other words, could
$$'\langle e_1,\text{Prhd},e_2\rangle e_1',$$
ever hold? The e_1 here would be the merest "puff of experience." Such a puff itself would undergo only *minimal* concrescence, but it could be ingredient in other concrescences. These concrescences would be minimal in the sense that the various "phases" would be degenerate. (A prehension that is its own subject is presumably the fusion of a unit class, that is, of a class whose only member is itself, a phase in general being a suitable fusion.)

Similarly forms such as
$$'\langle e,\text{Prhd},\alpha,e_1\rangle e',$$

and so on, could be admitted for conceptual prehensions that are their own subjects. And similarly with 'Prhd^i' in place of 'Prhd'. The admission of both physical and conceptual prehensions that are their own subjects seems not incompatible with Whitehead's actual text.

If such prehensions are admitted, then the *png* could be regarded as consisting of such only. It is then not *cng*'s conceptual valuations that give the primordial nature, but only those valuations that have themselves as their own subjects. Thus

'*png*' could now abbreviate 'Fu'$\hat{e}$(Ei)(Eα)(Ee_1)...(Ee_k)((($\langle e$,Prhd^i,α, $e_1\rangle e$ v ... v $\langle e$,Prhd^i,α,e_1...,$e_k\rangle e$) $\cdot$ e ϵ Val $\cdot$ $0 \leqq i \leqq 1$)'.

Prehensions that are their own subjects are genuinely "unconditioned" in the sense of undergoing only minimal or degenerate concrescence, in no way depending upon other prehensions or AO's. But they enter into other concrescences, of course, because the subjects of those concrescences prehend the primordial valuations.

Perhaps this third definition of '*png*' is the most satisfactory, and it will be presupposed in what follows.

It should be noted that, in view of the foregoing definitions, the *png* is a *part* of the *cng*, and hence of course God would be identified with the *cng* alone. It might be thought better to restrict the definition of '*cng*' in such a way that this would not hold and so that *cng* and *png* would be mutally exclusive. This could be done by letting

'*cng*' abbreviate 'Fu'$\hat{e}$ $\sim$ (Eμ)(*png* = Fu'μ $\cdot$ e ϵ μ)',
where 'μ' is some set variable. The *cng* in this way contains none of *png*'s valuations, although of course many of the valuations that it does contain may accord with them. This second definition also has the advantage of making the *cng* contain only "conditioned" prehensions, no "unconditioned" ones, and thus being more closely tied with the creative advance. Again, this second definition will be presupposed in what follows.

What now is God in his total fullness as comprising both his primordial and consequent natures? The logical sum of the two in the sense of the calculus of individuals. Thus,

'*God*' may now abbreviate '(*png* U *cng*)'.
In other words, *God* is *cng*, the fusion of the class of all actual entities, together with the fusion of all conceptual prehensions that are unconditioned and whose subjective forms are valuations. *God* is thus a highly complex entity with a very involved internal structure.

Is *God* an AO? Yes, he is a fusion of various prehensions, all such prehensions being AO's. In this way, *God* is not "treated as an exception to all metaphysical principles, invoked to save their collapse. He is their chief exemplification." He is an AO undergoing concrescence in the creative advance; one among many, but somewhat exceptional all the same owing to his unconditioned valuations and to his cumulativeness. On the consequent side, *God* is of course cumulative at any moment, containing the full cosmos up to that moment. Accordingly, when one speaks of *God's* prehensions one includes all prehensions, conceptual and physical, contained within him. And in general any entity in which all past entities are included may be said to prehend those entities.

Whenever God is mentioned hereafter, it should always be borne in mind precisely what is being referred to, whether just *png*, or rather *cng*, or *God* himself in his total fullness. Some of Whitehead's statements may seem puzzling if these three are not clearly distinguished. Some statements seem to refer primarily to one, others to another.

A word more concerning *God* and the sense in which he may be said to prehend or to be prehended. If neither the *cng* nor the *png* nor hence *God* are to be exceptions to metaphysical principles, expressions for them must of course be significant on either side of 'Prhd'. The question thus arises as to how '*cng* Prhd^i *e*', '*cng* Prhd^i α,*e*', and so on, as well as '*png* Prhd^i *e*', and so on, are to be interpreted. One way, which would seem to do no violence to Whitehead's doctrine, is to require perhaps that the following hold.[1]

$(e)(i)(cng$ Phrd^i $e \equiv e$ P $cng)$,

$(e)(\mathrm{E}i)png$ Prhd^i e,

$(\alpha)(e)(\mathrm{E}i)png$ Prhd^i α,*e*,

and so on. And thus that

$(e)(\mathrm{E}i)God$ Prhd^i e,

$(e)(\alpha)(\mathrm{E}i)God$ Prhd^i α,*e*,

and so on. (*i* here is of course between 0 and 1.)

---

[1] On various considerations relating to these and allied principles, see especially William Christian, *An Interpretation of Whitehead's Metaphysics* (Yale University Press, New Haven : 1959), esp. p. 396; Lewis Ford, "The Non-Temporality of Whitehead's God," *International Philosophical Quarterly* XIII (1973) : 347-376; and John Cobb, Jr., *A Christian Natural Theology* (Westminster Press, Philadelphia : 1965).

The question also arises as to the sense in which entities may be said to prehend *cng*, *png*, and *God*. Perhaps the following principles provide for this adequately.

$(e)(e$ P $cng \supset e$ Prhd^1 $cng)$,

$\sim (Ee)(E\alpha)(Re_1)(Ei)(\langle e, \text{Prhd}^i, \alpha, e_1 \rangle e \cdot e$ Prhd^1 $cng)$,

and so on, as well as that

$(e)(Ei)e$ Prhd^i *png*.

The use of numerical degrees here may seem a little foreign, but hopefully does no harm.

3

Let us comment now upon Chapter III, Section I, where God is first introduced in *Process and Reality*, in the light of the foregoing.

The "relevance" of an EO for a given AO is given or fixed in some primordial valuation. "There will be additional ground of relevance [p. 46] for select eternal objects by reason of their ingression into derivate actual entities belonging to the actual world of the concrescent occasion in question. But whether or not this is the case, there is always the definite relevance derived from God." A given AO may conceptually prehend EO's (relative to the AO's in its actual world) in modes other than just those of the *png*'s valuations of those EO's relative to those AO's. But no matter; each EO relative to all AO's is conceptually valuated to some degree in the *png*. "Apart from God, eternal objects unrealized in the actual world would be relatively non-existent for the concrescence in question," or for that matter for any concrescence. If an EO is null in the sense of never ingressing into any AO, in other words, "relatively non-existent," it at least fully "exists" in the sense of being a datum in one of the valuations of the *png*. "For effective relevance requires agency of comparison, and agency belongs exclusively to actual occasions." The "agent" is the "subject" in concrescence, and "effective relevance" is always that of an agent. The "ordering" of the valuations in the *png* is effective in the process of actuality and "has a real relevance to the creative advance."

"This divine ordering is itself matter of fact, thereby conditioning creativity." The valuations of the *png* in fact take place *in* and *with* the creative advance itself (p. 521). As metaphysical facts or principles we have then that

$(\alpha)(e_1)(\alpha \in EO^1 \supset (Ee)(Ei)(\langle e,Prhd^i,\alpha,e_1 \rangle e \cdot e \in Val \cdot 0 \leq i \leq 1))$,

$(\alpha)(e_1)(e_2)(\alpha \in EO^2 \supset (Ee)(Ei)(\langle e,Prhd^i,\alpha,e_1,e_2 \rangle e \cdot e \in Val \cdot 0 \leq i \leq 1))$,

and so on. These are *Principles of Existence* for *png*. In addition. *Principles of Uniqueness* are needed to assure that for each EO relative to given AO's there is *at most one* valuation of the desired kind of that EO relative to those AO's. More particularly,

$(\alpha)(e)(i)(e_1)(e')((\alpha \in EO^1 \cdot \langle e,Prhd^i,\alpha,e_1 \rangle e \cdot e \in Val \cdot \langle e',Prhd^i,\alpha,e_1 \rangle$ $e' \cdot e' \in Val \cdot 0 \leq i \leq 1) \supset e = e')$,

and so on, as well as

$(\alpha)(e)(e_1)(i)(i)((\alpha \in EO^1 \cdot \langle e,Prhd^i,\alpha,e_1 \rangle e \cdot \langle e,Prhd^j,\alpha,e_1 \rangle e \cdot e \in Val \cdot$ $0 \leq i \leq 1 \cdot 0 \leq j \leq 1) \supset i = j)$,

and so on. These principles of existence and uniqueness together assure us that the *png as a matter of metaphysical fact* contains uniquely the primordial valuations.

"Creativity" or the creative advance "is always found under conditions, and described as conditioned. The non-temporal act of all-inclusive unfettered valuation is at once a creature of creativity and a condition for creativity. It shares this double character with all creatures." The *png* is both a creature, being a fusion of prehensions, and a "condition for creativity," being the primordial "lure for feeling." Each AO is a creature and also a condition for creativity in the sense of being in the "actual world" of every subsequent concrescence. The *png* is a "non-temporal act" in the sense of being an "integrated" prehension so complex that to attempt to locate it spatio-temporally would be hopelessly difficult if not impossible. "By reason of its [*God's*] character as a creature, always in concrescence and never wholly in the past, it receives a reaction from the world; this reaction is its consequent nature." The *png* is operative in each concrescence and each concrescence is a "reaction" to it. The *cng* is never wholly in the past, but is always being augmented with each new concrescence.

The *cng* is appropriately a part of *God*, and so-called, "because the comtemplation of our natures, as enjoying real feelings derived from the timeless source [valuation] of all order, acquires that 'subjective form' of refreshment and companionship at which religions aim." This "refreshment and companionship" is for Whitehead a matter of fact, not of conjecture. Perhaps not everyone feels them, but some at least do, as a matter of fact. Let 'Refr' and 'Cmpn' stand respectively for the subjective forms of the kind of consciously-felt refreshment and companionship "at which religions aim." Then

$(Ee)(Ee')(Ee'')(E\alpha)(Ee_1)...(Ee_k)(Ei)((\langle e',\text{Prhd}^i,\alpha,e_1\rangle e' \; v \; ... \; v \; \langle e',$
$\text{Prhd}^i,\alpha,e_1,...,e_k\rangle e') \cdot e' \; \epsilon \; \text{Val} \cdot 0 \leqq i \leqq 1 \cdot \langle e,\text{Prhd}^i,e'\rangle e'' \cdot (e'' \; \epsilon$
$\text{Refr} \; v \; e'' \; \epsilon \; \text{Cmpn})).$

That this and allied principles concerning religious experience hold
for Whitehead is eloquent testimony that God is needed in his system
in a most fundamental way. To excise him, as some have attempted
to do, is to alter the system unrecognizably and to allow no place
for principles that are integral to the system and not mere appendages.

A word more concerning the "non-temporal" character of the *png*.
It was suggested a moment back that to attempt to locate the *png* in the
temporal flow would be hopelessly difficult if not impossible. The
reason is that the valuations constituting the *png* are "unconditioned."
More needs to be said about this, but only after physical time and
space have been introduced into the system. In any case, the *png* is
presumably the *only* non-temporal creature, and the doctrine of spatio-
temporal order must be so arranged that this circumstance is in no
way exceptional but rather a "chief exemplification" of it.

"This function of creatures, that they constitute the shifting character of creativity, is here termed the 'objective immortality' of actual
entities. Thus God has objective immortality in respect to [both] his
primordial nature and his consequent nature." The objective immortality of an AO may be regarded as, put loosely, just the fusion of the
class of all the prehensions (physical or conceptual) that are borne
e by something or other, as in I above. The objective immortality
of the *png* is then just the *png* itself, for all its constituent valuations
are prehended to some degree by all AO's. The objective immortality
of the *cng* likewise may be regarded as just the *cng* itself, for all its
constituent AO's other than itself are prehended by some *e* or other
to at least some degree.

4

Let us comment now on the most significant passages in the last
chapter, "God and the World" (*Process and Reality*, pp. 519-533),
especially Sections II ff., in the light of the foregoing.

"Viewed as primordial," Whitehead notes again (p. 521), God
"is the unlimited conceptual realization of the absolute wealth of
potentiality." The use of 'conceptual valuation' would perhaps be
better here than 'conceptual realization'. Potentialities become realized
only with actualization. The *png* however, involves no actualization,

only valuations. "In this aspect he is not *before* all creation, but *with* all creation." Clearly the *png* is not before all creation, for strictly he cannot be spoken of relative to time at all. In what sense now is the *png with* all creation? Just in the sense that "there is an order in the relevance of eternal objects to the process of creation," as already noted. The *png*'s "unity of conceptual operations is a free creative act, untrammelled by reference to any particular course of things." Thus

$$(e)((e \in \text{CncptlPrhn} \cdot e \text{ P } png) \supset e \in \text{Dcsn}_e).$$

Every conceptual prehension that is a part of the *png* is a free decision by some entity, namely itself. These valuations are "deflected neither by love, nor by hatred, nor what in fact comes to pass." If they were, they would be conditioned by the physical world, whereas it is the *ideality* or the *png* that is relevant here.

"The *particularities* of the actual world presuppose *it* [the *png*]; while *it* merely presupposes the general character of creative advance, of which it is the primordial exemplification." The AO's presuppose the realm of order — no EO's, no concrescences. On the other hand, the *png* involves the unconditioned valuations of the EO's, and it is the EO's that determine "the general character of creative advance." Finally, the *png* is the "primordial exemplification" of this general character in the sense that it consists after all of the "unfettered" valuations of all EO's and not of anything less.

The *png* is of course "deficiently actual" in comprising no physical feelings, and also in lacking consciousness. A prehension is conscious, it will be recalled, when it is "integrated" with a physical prehension. Thus

$$\sim (Ee)(e \in \text{PhysPrhn} \cdot e \text{ P } png)$$

and

$$\sim png \in \text{Cnsc},$$

whereas

$$cng \in \text{Cnsc}.$$

The *png*, although devoid of actuality, is of course replete with ideality. The *png* is, strictly, God's eternal vision of the ideal order of the cosmos. The valuations comprising the *png* "exemplify in their subjective forms their mutual sensitivity and their subjective unity of subjective aim." The "unity of subjective aim" is provided by the principle that the cosmos as a whole always has as its subjective aim the "realization" of the valuations of the *png*. Thus, we have principles of cosmic aim — to the effect that

$(e_1)...(e_n)(\alpha)(i)((Ee')(e' \epsilon \text{Val} \cdot 0 \leq i \leq 1 \cdot \langle e',\text{Prhd}^i,\alpha,e_1,...,e_n\rangle e') \supset$
$(Ee'')(e'' \epsilon \text{SA}_{cng} \cdot \langle cng,\text{Prhd}^i,\alpha,e_1,...,e_n\rangle e''))$,
and so on, for each n $(1 \leq n \leq k)$. The valuations are mutually harmonious with the one unified subjective aim no doubt of achieving maximal realization of truth, beauty, and goodness, and all derivative excellences. In any case, these valuations determine, in the sense of providing "the lure for feeling, the eternal urge [better perhaps, object] of desire," the "relative relevance [or degree of relevance or value] for each occasion of actuality." Each occasion in actuality prehends each eternal object as it will, but in ideality always values each eternal object to just the degree that it is valued unconditionally. However, there is always failure of actual achievement in this regard, as recorded by the following principles, for each n $(1 \leq n \leq k)$.

$(Ee')(E\alpha)(Ee_1)...(Ee_n)(Ei)(e' \epsilon \text{Val} \cdot (i > 0 \cdot \langle e',\text{Prhd}^i,\alpha,e_1,...,e_n\rangle e'$
$\cdot \sim \alpha \text{ Ing } e_1,...,e_n) \text{ v } (i = 0 \cdot \langle e',\text{Prhd}^i,\alpha,e_1,...,e_n\rangle e' \cdot \alpha \text{ Ing } e_1,...,e_n))$.
These existence laws provide for the presence of evil in the cosmos.

The *png* is thus relevant to each creative act [i.e., decisional conceptual prehension] as it arises from its own conditioned standpoint in the world" and constitutes "the initial 'object of desire' establishing the initial phase of each subjective aim." In other words, each AO, no matter what its standpoint in the world, values initially each EO precisely as it is valued unconditionally. Thus

$(e)(e_1)...(e_n)(\alpha)(i)((Ee')(e' \epsilon \text{Val} \cdot 0 \leq i \leq 1 \cdot \langle e',\text{Prhd}^i,\alpha,e_1,...,e_n\rangle e')$
$\supset (Ee')(e' \epsilon \text{Val} \cdot \langle e,\text{Prhd}^i,\alpha,e_1,...,e_n\rangle e'))$,
for each n $(1 \leq n \leq k)$. Further, it has as its subjective aims the purpose to realize that valuation in its own concrescence. Thus also

$(e)(e_1)...(e_n)(\alpha)(i)((Ee')(e' \epsilon \text{Val} \cdot 0 \leq i \leq 1 \cdot \langle e',\text{Prhd}^i,\alpha,e_1,...,e_n\rangle e')$
$\supset (Ee')(e' \epsilon \text{SA}_e \cdot \langle e,\text{Prhd}^i,\alpha,e_1,...,e_n\rangle e'))$.
Of course it may not actually succeed in realizing this subjective aim, and it is free not to choose even to try to do so if it so wishes. Again, evil prevails, and as a result of one of e's decisions. Thus

$(Ee)(Ee')(E\alpha)(Ee_1)...(Ee_u)(Ei)(e' \epsilon \text{Val} \cdot 0 \leq i \leq 1 \cdot \langle e',\text{Prhd}^i,\alpha,$
$e_1,...,e_n\rangle e' \cdot \sim (Ee'')(e'' \epsilon \text{Dcsn}_e \cdot \langle e,\text{Prhd}^i,\alpha,e_1,...,e_n\rangle e''))$.
Each EO is lured by the valuations in the *png* but is free to do and decide as it will; and some reject that lure.

5

The *png* acts on the world as "the principle of concretion — the principle whereby there is initiated a definite outcome from a situation otherwise riddled with ambiguity." The "situation ... riddled with ambiguity" is perhaps the entire multiplicity of eternal objects with no unconditioned valuations thereon. For any given AO, the "definite outcome," that is, its conceptual valuation of a given EO, may or may not accord with the unconditioned valuations with respect to that EO. But in any case, there is present the "lure for feeling," the object of desire, guiding with gentle persuasiveness and love the actual valuation to accord with the ideal one. Without such guidance, the concrescence is "riddled with ambiguity" and confusion, not knowing what valuations to make nor why.

The *cng*, unlike the *png*, "is the beginning and the end," and the middle as well. "He is not the beginning in the sense of being in the past of all members." He is the beginning in the sense that given any *e*, the *cng^e* (the whole cosmos anterior to and including *e*) is an initial part of the *cng* itself. And similarly he is the end in the sense that given any *e*, the

$$\text{Fu}^{\mathfrak{e}'}(\sim e' \text{ P } cng^e \cdot \sim (E\mu)(png = \text{Fu}^{\mathfrak{e}}\mu \cdot e' \epsilon \mu))$$

is a part of the *cng* itself.

"He is the presupposed actuality of conceptual operation, in unison of becoming with every other creative act. Thus by reason of the relativity of all things, there is a reaction of the world on God." The *cng* "becomes" in the sense that every concrescence is a part of it, and the whole "becomes" with the becoming of each and every one of its parts. And the *cng* is "the presupposed actuality of conceptual operation" of any AO in the sense that all antecedent AO's with their completed conceptual prehensions are themselves parts of it. Each EO "presupposes" all such conceptual prehensions. There is "a reaction of the world on God" in the sense that the entire cosmos *up to* any *e* in also a part of the *cng*. Each *e* is of course objectively immortal in the *cng*, and the "completion of God's nature into a fullness of physical feeling," the *cng* itself, "is derived from the objectification [objective immortality] of the world [up to any *e*] in God." Also he "shares with every new creation its actual world; and the concrescent creature is objectified in God as a novel element in God's objectification of that actual world." Clearly the actual world of any new *e* is a part of the *cng*, as is *e* itself. "This prehension into [inclusion in] God of each creature [p. 16] is directed with the subjective aim, and clothed with the subjective form, wholly derivative from his all-inclusive primordial valuation." The use of 'prehension into God' here is merely informal. Each concrescence has the primordial valuations available as a lure for feeling, even if it heeds them not. The all-inclusive "conceptual nature [*png*] is unchanged by reason of its final completeness. But his derivative nature [*cng*] is consequent upon the creative advance of the world." Clearly the *png* is fixed once and for all. Of course the *cng* is also fixed in the sense of including all *e* whatsoever. On the other hand, the *cng* contains within its "real internal constitution" each concrescence and in this sense depends upon them.

The sum *God*, (*png* ∪ *cng*), is genuinely dipolar, just as each AO is. Each AO is dipolar in the sense of being a concrescence of both physical and conceptual feelings. "The consequent nature of God is conscious; and it is the realization of the actual world in the unity of his nature, and through the transformation of his wisdom." The consciousness of the *cng* is dependent upon the consciousness of its parts and arises only with the integration of physical with conceptual feelings. Thus only the *cng* can be said to be conscious, not the *png*, devoid as it is of physical feelings. This has been noted above. "The primordial nature is conceptual, the consequent nature is the weaving of God's physical feelings upon his primordial concepts," where 'weaving' is taken to express the integration of physical and conceptual prehensions.

The *png* is "infinite, devoid of all negative prehensions." It is infinite in the sense that it is "limited by no actuality which it presupposes." It is "free, complete, primordial, eternal, actually deficient, and unconscious." It is free in the sense of consisting of all the unconditioned valuations. It is complete in the sense that the valuation of *every* eternal object is a part of it. It is eternal in the sense of being fixed once and for all. It is actually deficient, as already noted, in involving only conceptual feelings, and unconscious in involving no complex feelings integrated with physical ones. The *cng*, on the other hand, is "determined, incomplete, consequent, 'everlasting', fully actual, and conscious" — determined in the sense of consisting of AO's, the finite determined actualities, incomplete in the sense of not containing at any given time all AO's but of increasing continually with the creative advance of the cosmos, "everlasting" in the sense that given any AO there is always an AO that prehends it and one that it prehends (everlasting in the future as well as in the past), *fully* actual in the sense of comprising all actualities, and conscious of course in the sense of containing integrated conceptual and physical prehensions from which consciousness can arise. "His necessary goodness expresses the determination of his consequent nature," the subjective aim, that is, of each AO to make its primary valuations in accord with those of the *png*.

"Conceptual experience can be infinite" in the sense of not being limited by actuality, "but it belongs to the nature of physical experience that it is finite" in the sense of being thus limited. "An actual entity in the temporal world is to be conceived as originated by physical experience initially derived from God." A concrescence consists of both physical and conceptual prehensions, the latter being always available as the primordial lure for feeling. On the other hand, "God is to be conceived as originated by conceptual experience with his process of completion motivated by consequent, physical experience, initially derived from the temporal world." God seems fundamentally to be the *png* but fully or completed only with adding as a logical summand the *cng*. No special significance should be attached in these two sentences to Whitehead's use of 'originated by', 'consequent', or 'initially derived'. They could be deleted without loss of content.

6

A "perfect" valuation is one in accord with those of the *png*. Thus
'$e \in$ PerfVal' may abbreviate '($e \in$ Val $\cdot$ (Ee')(Eα)(Ee_1)...(Ee_k)(Ei)(e'
$\in$ Val $\cdot 0 \leq i \leq 1 \cdot ((\langle e',\mathrm{Prhd}^i,\alpha,e_1\rangle e' \cdot (\mathrm{E}e'')\langle e'',\mathrm{Prhd}^i,\alpha,e_1\rangle e) \mathrm{v} ... \mathrm{v}$
$(\langle e,\mathrm{Prhd}^i,\alpha,e_1,...,e_k\rangle e' \cdot (\mathrm{E}e'')\langle e'',\mathrm{Prhd}^i,\alpha,e_1,...,e_k\rangle e))))$'.
Similarly, a "perfect" subjective aim is one in accord with those of the *png*. Thus
'$e' \in$ PerfSA$_e$' abbreviates '($e' \in$ SA$_e$ $\cdot$ (Ee'')(Eα)(Ee_1)...(Ee_k)(Ei)(e''
$\in$ Val $\cdot 0 \leq i \leq 1 \cdot ((\langle e'',\mathrm{Prhd}^i,\alpha,e_1\rangle e'' \cdot \langle e,\mathrm{Prhd}^i,\alpha,e_1\rangle e') \mathrm{v} ... \mathrm{v}$
$(\langle e'',\mathrm{Prhd}^i,\alpha,e_1,...,e_k\rangle e'' \cdot \langle e,\mathrm{Prhd}^i,\alpha,e_1,...,e_k\rangle e'))))$'.

"The wisdom of [the primordial] subjective aim [p. 525] prehends every actuality for what it can be [even this wisdom being limited by the physical factors] in such a perfected system— its sufferings, its sorrows, its failures, its triumphs, its immediacies of joy — woven by rightness of feeling into the harmony of the universal feeling, which is always immediate, always many, always one, always with novel advance, moving onward and never perishing," This famous sentence is not to be interpreted as saying that the "wisdom" of the *png* sees no evil, but only that the evil is absorbed by and harmonized into the ever emerging universal feeling. "The revolts of destructive evil, purely self-regarding, are dismissed into their triviality of merely individual facts; and yet the good they did achieve in individual joy, in individual sorrow, in the introduction of needed contrast, is yet saved by its relation to the completed whole." Every concrescence becomes absorbed in the *cng*, as do all valuations (other than the primordial ones), all rejoicings, all sorrowings, and so on. Each is thereafter ever present to be valuated in accord with the valuations of the *png*. Such valuations "save" the temporal world and future valuations may yet accord with those of the *png*, even if past ones have not.

"The consequent nature of God is his judgment on the world. He saves the world as it passes into the immediacy of his own life. It is the judgment of a tenderness which loses nothing that can be saved. It is also the judgment of a wisdom which uses what in the temporal world is mere wreckage." The *cng* receives each item of the passing world into its real internal constitution. This reception is the "judgment," the saving "tenderness" that preserves each AO in its status of having been just what it was, even if mere "wreckage." All AO's are "covered" by the *cng* as creatures in its internal nature. Whitehead speaks of the "infinite patience" of the *cng*. What he says of it indicates that he means to refer rather to the infinite patience of *God*. "The universe includes a threefold creative act" composed of (i) the *png*, (ii) all purely physical prehensions, the *World*, and (iii) the *cng*. "If we conceive the first term and the last term in their unity over against the intermediate multiple freedom of physical realizations in the temporal world, we conceive of the patience of God, tenderly saving the turmoil of the intermediate world by the completion of his own nature ... [God] does not create the world, he saves it" by receiving it into his own real internal constitution; "or, more accurately, he is the poet of the world, with tender patience leading it by his vision of truth, beauty, and goodness" incorporated in the primordial valuations.

7

The final summary as to the interrelations between flux (or "fluency") and permanence, the one and the many, immanence and transcendence, and creation is given by Whitehead in the six "antitheses" (p. 528) concerning God and the World.

"It is as true that God is permanent and the World fluent, as that the World in permanent and God is fluent." The use of 'is as true

that' here is insignificant, for all that is asserted is presumably intended
to be true. For God to be permanent is for him to contain all and
only the primordial valuations, and for the World to be permanent
is for it to contain *all* physical prehensions. On the other hand, both
the World and *God* are fluent in the sense of containing at least one
(fluent) concrescence. Let

'$e \in$ PrimVal' abbreviate '$(e \in$ Val $\cdot (E\alpha) (Ee_1)...(Ee_k)(Ei)(0 \leq i \leq 1 \cdot (\langle e, \text{Prhd}^i, \alpha, e_1 \rangle e$ v ... v $\langle e, \text{Prhd}^i, \alpha, e_1,...,e_k \rangle e)))$'.
Then

$(e)(e \in$ PrimVal $\supset e$ P $png) \cdot (Ee)(e \in$ AO $\cdot e$ P $God) \cdot (e)(e \in$ Phys Prhn $\supset e$ P $World) \cdot (Ee)(e \in$ PhysPrhn $\cdot e$ P $World)$.
where

'*World*' abbreviates 'Fu'PhysPrhn'.

"It is as true to say that God is one and the World many, as that
the World is one and God many." God is one in the sense that both
the *cng* and the *png* are unique fusions and hence that (*cng* ∪ *png*)
is, and the World is one in the sense that the fusion of the class of
physical prehensions is also unique. On the other hand, both the
World and God are many in the sense of containing at least two
concrescences.

World = Fu'PhysPrhn $\cdot$ *God* = (*cng* ∪ *png*) $\cdot (Ee_1)(Ee_2)(e_1$ P *World* $\cdot e_2$ P *World* $\cdot \sim e_1 = e_2) \cdot (Ee_1)(Ee_2)(e_1$ P *God* $\cdot e_2$ P *God* $\cdot \sim e_1 = e_2)$.

"It is as true to say that, in comparison with the World, God is
actual eminently, as that, in comparison with God, the World is
actual eminently." God is "actual eminently" in the sense of containing all concrescences, but the World is not, in the sense of not
being conscious. On the other hand, the World is eminently actual
in the sense of containing all physical prehensions, whereas the *png*
lacks eminent actuality because it contains none such.

$(e)e$ P $God \cdot \sim$ *World* $\in$ Cnsc $\cdot (e)(e \in$ PhysPrhn $\supset e$ P *World*) $\cdot \sim (Ee)(e \in$ PhysPrhn $\cdot e$ P $png)$.

"It is as true to say that the World is immanent in God, as that God
is immanent in the World." The World is "immanent" in God in
the sense of bearing P to it. And God is "immanent" in the World
in the sense of supplying the initial SA's for all concrescences. Thus

World P *God* $\cdot (e)(Ee')(e' \in$ SA$_e \cdot e'$ P $png)$.

"It is as true to say that God transcends the World as that the
World transcends God." Clearly God contains prehensions not includ-

ed in the World, and the World contains prehensions not included in the *png*.

$(Ee)(e \,\epsilon\, \text{Prhn} \cdot e \,P\, God \cdot \sim e \,P\, World) \cdot (Ee)(e \,\epsilon\, \text{Prhn} \cdot e \,P\, World \cdot \sim e \,P\, png)$.

"It is as true to say that God creates the world as to say that the World creates God." God "creates" the World in the sense of providing items in it with the initial valuations or subjective aims, but the World creates God in the sense of providing the physical data for those valuations. Thus

$(e)(e \,\epsilon\, \text{PrimVal} \supset (e \,\epsilon\, \text{Val} \cdot (Ee')e \,\epsilon\, SA_e')) \cdot (e)(e \,P\, World \supset (Ee')(E\alpha)(e_1)...(Ee_k) \, (Ei)(e' \,\epsilon\, \text{Val} \cdot 0 \leq i \leq 1 \cdot ((\langle e',\text{Prhd}^i,\alpha,e_1\rangle e' \cdot e = e_1) \,v\, ... \,v\, (\langle e',\text{Prhd}^i,\alpha,e_1,...,e_k\rangle e' \cdot (e' = e_1 \,v\, ... \,v\, e = e_k)))))$.

The renditions given of these six "antitheses" are by no means the only ones, the antitheses themselves being highly ambiguous.

It might seem "philistine to lay the rude hands of logic" — C. I. Lewis' phrase — upon a subject so lofty as the "real internal constitution" of God. It should not be forgotten however, that Whitehead for most of his adult life was a professional mathematician, and it is interesting to note that even when he writes about God the movement of his thought is that of a mathematician, first giving definitions and then theorems based on them. Especially important are the definitions. From the strict point of view of just developing a logical system, the definitions are regarded merely as notational conventions of abbreviation. However, as Whitehead himself pointed out in an early writing,[2] "... if we abandon the strictly logical point of view, the definitions ... are at once seen to be the most important part of the subject. The act ... [of giving a definition] ... is in fact the act of choosing the various complex ideas which are to be the special object of study. The whole subject depends upon such a choice." Once the definitions have been chosen, the derivation of theorems should come out easily enough in terms of previously proved theorems, the axioms, and of course the principles of the underlying logic.

It is interesting to note that in the foregoing the definitions have been crucial. Alternatives have been suggested and it is not always clear which ones are preferable for the intended purposes. Also various metaphysical principles have been suggested, in addition to those required (in I above) for the categoreal scheme. Some of these, or

[2] *The Axioms of Projective Geometry* (Cambridge University Press, Cambridge : 1906), p. 2.

similar ones, might be suitable to take as axioms. Strictly the axioms and definitions go hand in hand and should be given together. To suggest a suitable set of axioms for the whole of the Whiteheadian cosmology, however, would be a formidable task indeed. Meanwhile, the tentative definitions and comments above may be useful as a first step in helping to clarify the logical structure of Whitehead's theory of God. The exhibition of such structure is not only an aid to understanding, it is so important in fact that without it we can scarcely be said to know what that theory really is.

IV

ON COORDINATE DIVISIONS
IN THE THEORY OF EXTENSIVE CONNECTION

"DE NON APPARENTIBUS ET DE NON EXISTENTIBUS EADEM EST RATIO."

Pages 436-8 (comprising Section II of Chapter I, "Coordinate Division," of Part IV, "The Theory of Extension") of Whitehead's *Process and Reality*, are perhaps the most difficult in this notoriously difficult book. The pages are crucial, however, for an understanding of the difference between an actual entity and a coordinate division. It is by means of the latter "entities," if such they be, that Whitehead seeks to accommodate the foundations of geometry. Let us try to determine precisely what coordinate divisions are supposed to be, according to Whitehead, for these constitute the basic kind of entity in the theory of extensive connection. Whitehead's own statements here are highly obscure and unsatisfactory. In examining them afresh by way of an *explication de texte*, we may be in a position to suggest an interpretation that would be viable on Whitehead's own grounds and even perhaps to help pave the way for an adequate theory as to what geometry is.

There are two ways of dividing the satisfaction of an actual entity [AO or AE], it will be recalled, genetic and coordinate. Genetic division (pp. 433-4) is division of an AO into the component prehensions of its concrescence; coordinate division of an AO, the "parent entity," is concerned with the "enjoyment" of that AO with "a certain quantum of physical time," which also contains "a spatial element." This spatio-temporal quantum is "an extensive region." These regions are the relata of the relations EC, for being extensively connected with, presumably the only primitive relation of the theory.

Whitehead must be taken at his word that the only fundamental entities of the theory are AO's (including prehensions) and eternal objects (EO's) and that all others are derivative. Extensive regions are thus not to be a new entity but must be handled somehow in terms of what is already available. Where 'e', 'e_1', 'e_2', 'e'', and so on, are variables for AO's, the form

$$'e_1 \text{ EC } e_2'$$

may be allowed now to express that the "region" of the AO e_1 is extensively connected with the "region" of the AO e_2. In this way, no new entities are admitted in the transition to the theory of extensive connection, and much of the latter can be accommodated.

A difficulty emerges, however, when we come to the notion of a coordinate division (CD). A CD is not an AO (nor of course an EO), nor is it strictly a "region." A CD rather is a "sub-region" or subdivision of a region.

"Each ... coordinate division corresponds to a definite sub-region of the basic region," Whitehead writes (p. 436). "It expresses that component of the satisfaction which has the character of a unified feeling of the actual world from the standpoint of that sub-region. In so far as the objectification of the actual world from this restricted standpoint is concerned, there is nothing to distinguish this coordinate division from an actual entity. But it is only the physical pole which is thus divisible. The mental pole is incurably one. Thus the subjective form of this coordinate division is derived from the origination of conceptual feelings which have regard to the complete region, and are not restricted to the sub-region in question. In other words, the conceptual feelings have regard to the complete actual entity, and not to the coordinate division in question. ... It is obvious that in so far as the mental pole is trivial as to originality, what is inexplicable in the coordinate divison (taken as actually separate) becomes thereby trivial. Thus for many abstractions concerning low-grade actual entities, the coordinate divisions approach the character of being actual entities on the same level as the actual entity from which they are derived."

This passage assures us that a CD (i) is "derived" from a "parent" AO e, (ii) has to do primarily with e's physical pole, (iii) shares e's mental pole (with some eliminations), and (iv) corresponds to a sub-region of the basic region of e. This is not very illuminating, however, unless we are given an exact description of just what a "derivation" here consists of, of just how the CD's physical and mental poles differ from those of e if at all, and of just what a sub-region is and how it arises from the basic region. And all this must be done in terms of just the ontology already available, as Whitehead would most surely insist.

The paragraphs that follow on the crucial page 437 are supposed presumably to provide these descriptions. "It is thus an empirical question to decide in relation to special topics, whether the distinction between a coordinate division and a true actual entity [CD's not being quite "true" AO's] is, or is not, relevant. In so far as it is not relevant [as for low-grade AO's] we are dealing with an indefinitely subdivisible extensive universe." The suggestion here is that in dealing with low-grade entities, we are dealing with entities whose regions can be indefinitely subdivided and that such entities "approach the character" of being AO's "on the same level" as the parent AO's. But the regions corresponding to high-grade entities are also presumably coordinately divisible — we are nowhere told that they are not — so that even where the distinction between a CD and a true AO is relevant, we also are dealing with "an indefinitely subdivisible extensive universe." This paragraph is thus of little help in distinguishing CD's from true AO's.

The next two paragraphs attempt to make amends. "A coordinate division is ... to be classed as a generic contrast," we are told, as though a definition were in the offing. "The two components of the contrast are, (i) the parent actual entity, and (ii) the proposition which is the potentiality of that superject having arisen from the physical standpoint of the restricted sub-region. The proposition is thus the potentiality of eliminating from the physical pole of the parent entity all the objectified actual world [of the parent entity], except those elements derivable from that standpoint; and yet retaining the relevant elements of the subjective form." According to this, a CD is presumably an ordered couple of a "parent" AO with a certain proposition. Would that Whitehead had given us the precise form of this proposition! It is supposed to state that the superject, that is, here the parent AO regarded as a completed concrescence, could arise — could undergo concrescence — from the physical standpoint of "the restricted sub-region." What sub-region? Some imaginary one presumably of the region of the parent AO. Whitehead has no right to speak of a sub-region here *without telling us what it is and how it arises*. Strictly there is no ontology of regions available, let alone one including subregions.

The proposition here is spoken of as a "potentiality" but presumably what is meant is that such and such *could* take place. Usually when Whitehead speaks of a "potentiality" or of a "potential" he means merely an EO. His doctrine of "necessity in universality" reinforces this contention, especially when brought into connection with the universal quantifiers. There is little reason to think that Whitehead ever uses 'potential' or 'potentiality' in any other sense.

Let us reflect now upon the remainder of Whitehead's text, the following two paragraphs, the only additional ones throwing light on this subject.

"The unqualified proposition [constituting the second member of the pair comprising a CD] is false, because the mental pole, which is in fact operative, would not be the mental pole under the hypothesis [supposition — there is no suggestion that the proposition should be of hypothetical form] of the proposition. But, for many purposes, the falsity of the proposition is irrelevant. The proposition is very complex; and with the relevant qualifications depending on the topic in question, it expresses the truth. In other words, the unqualified false proposition is a matrix from which an indefinite number of true qualified propositions can be derived. The requisite qualification depends on the special topic in question, and expresses the limits of the application of the unqualified proposition relevantly to that topic." The last paragraph, finally, tells us that the "unqualified proposition expresses the indefinite divisibility of the actual world; the qualifications express the features of the world which are lost sight of by the unguarded use of this principle. The actual world is atomic; but in some senses it is indefinitely divisible." These two paragraphs are not among Whitehead's most felicitous, but it is imperative that we try to make sense of them.

It has been suggested elsewhere that sentences containing subjunctives, 'could be's, and so on, can be handled in pragmatics by bringing in the speaker and some propositional attitude.[1] In Whitehead's system propositional attitudes are the subjective forms of propositional prehensions. The 'could be' kind of clause can thus be handled by requiring that someone (more specifically, some AO) propositionally prehend the proposition in question. Let

$$\text{'}e \text{ PrpnPrhd } \mu\text{'}$$

express that e propositionally prehends μ, as in I above.

The problem now is to consider precisely what form the relevant proposition may take. The only clues Whitehead has given us, it will be recalled, it that the superject could arise "from the

---

[1] See especially "A Plethora of Logical Forms" in *Events, Reference, and Logical Form*.

physical standpoint of the restricted sub-region," yet "retaining the relevant elements of the subjective form." To accommodate these two requirements, consider a "parent" entity e_1 and another one e_2. If every AO that e_1 physically prehends positively is also physically prehended positively by e_2, and for every subjective form β, if there is one of e_2's prehensions that has β and is a part of the satisfaction of e_2, then there is one of e_1's prehensions that has β and is a part of the satisfaction of e_1, where e_2 is a part of e_1 but e_1 is not a part of e_2. These four requirements, as conjoined in a proposition propositionally prehended by some AO, seem to capture what is needed. The AO e_1 could have arisen (as entertained in some propositional prehension) from the physical standpoint of e_2 in the sense that everything the former physically prehends positively the latter is regarded as doing also. Likewise e_2 retains the "relevant" elements of the subjective form of e_1 in the sense that every subjective form of one of e_2's prehensions is regarded as the subjective form of one of e_1's also. And further, e_2 is regarded as a part of e_1 but e_2 is not regarded as a part of e_2. Note the use of 'is regarded as' here to remind us that the proposition (and thus its components) are merely prehended and not necessarily true. The subjective form of this propositional prehension is not given; presumably it is that of conjecture, or of being conceived as, or merely taken as (even if falsely).

In short, we may let

'ν CD e_1' abbreviate '$(\nu = \langle e_1, \hat{\mu}(E\alpha)(Ee_2)(Ee_3)(\mu = \langle \alpha, e_1, e_2 \rangle \cdot (\alpha e_1 e_2 \equiv (e_2 \text{ P } e_1 \cdot \sim e_1 \text{ P } e_2 \cdot (e)(e_1 \,^+\text{Prhd } e \supset e_2 \,^+\text{Prhd } e) \cdot (\beta)((\beta \in \text{SF} \cdot (Ee)(e \in \beta \cdot e \text{ Prhn } e_2 \cdot e \text{ P Sat}'e_2)) \supset (Ee)(e \in \beta \cdot e \text{ Prhn } e_1 \cdot e \text{ P Sat}'e_1)))) \cdot e_3 \text{ PropPrhn } \mu)\rangle)$'.

The definiendum reads 'ν is a coordinate division of e_1 as the parent entity'.

Concerning CD, assumptions must be made, in particular that, given any e_1, there are non-countably many ν's such that ν CD e_1.

Whitehead states that the "unqualified" proposition here is "false, because the mental pole, which is in fact operative, would [could(?)] not be the mental pole under the hypothesis of the proposition." The mental pole of what AO? Of e_3, perhaps. And what does 'unqualified' here mean? Merely as not taken under the given propositional attitude. Clearly μ must be false because in fact the mental pole of each AO is "incurably" one.

At work here is a Principle of the Incurable Unity of the Subjective Forms of the Satisfaction in the Mental Pole :

$(e_1)(e_2)((\beta)((\beta \in SF \cdot (Ee)(e \in \beta \cdot e \text{ CncptlPrhn } e_2 \cdot e \text{ P Sat}'e_2)) \supset$
$(Ee)(e \in \beta \cdot e \text{ CncptlPrhn } e_1 \cdot e \text{ P Sat}'e_1)) \supset e_1 = e_2).$

On the other hand, the "qualified" proposition, that some e_3 propositionally prehends μ, is true and functions as a "matrix from which an indefinite number of true ... propositions can be derived." These true propositions are to the effect that e_3 propositionally prehends the various conjuncts of μ, so to speak, as well as instantiated instances of those that contain quantifiers.

The "special topics" of which Whitehead speaks here are of course those of the foundations of geometry, of the theory of flat loci and of strains, and of the theory of measurement. These subjects have to do with "abstractions concerning low-grade entities" *regarded as* approaching "the character of being actual entities on the same level as the actual entity from which they are derived."

The concern here has not been merely to attempt an *explication de texte* of a few of Whitehead's most obscure pages, for their relevance extends far beyond to many issues under contemporary discussion. Involved is a method of handling subjunctive conditionals, statements of modality, and the like, of a far-reaching generality. Underlying the treatment is an event logic of wide applicability to physics, to linguistics, to arithmetic and geometry, and of course to general metaphysics. And any atomic theory of reality in which physical geometry plays an integral role must come up against the problem as to how idealized geometric elements arise or can be "derived" from the fundamental atoms. The mode of treatment suggested thus far transcends the confines of interest in Whitehead's system. Geometric elements come out as mere fictions in some sense and it is important to know exactly how. "The actual world is atomic; but in some sense it is indefinitely divisible." There may be many such senses, but we are fortunate if we can succeed in characterizing adequately at least one.

V

ON ABSTRACTIVE HIERARCHIES

"Etiam capillus unus habet umbram suam."

In the chapter "Abstraction," in *Science and the Modern World*,[1] Whitehead puts forward what he calls "the first chapter in metaphysics." This gives an "account of an actual occasion in terms of its connection with the realm of eternal objects" and harks back to the "train of thought" in a previous chapter "where the nature of mathematics was discussed." More specifically, what Whitehead calls the "analytical character of the realm of eternal objects," which is "the primary mataphysical truth concerning it," is characterized in this chapter in quasi-mathematical terms. We seek in vain in later writings for a more detailed and careful statement as to how eternal objects are interrelated amongst themselves. Therefore this chapter on "Abstraction" seems to contain the key to understanding one very important aspect of the later cosmology. In fact, it has been called "the basic text for the doctrine of eternal objects."[2] Unfortunately this difficult chapter is usually neglected by commentators, and some of Whitehead's ablest followers say that they have not understood it.

Let us examine the text of this chapter in detail (especially pp. 236-248), bearing in mind the doctrine of types in *Principia Mathematica*. We shall see that there is a close formal affinity between type theory and the "analytical character of the realm of eternal objects." This suggests that Whitehead very likely was presupposing type theory as the underlying logic for his later cosmology, even though he makes no essential use of it there.

By the "*analytical character* of the realm of eternal objects ...,"

[1] (The Macmillan Co., New York : 1925), pp. 226-248.
[2] Charles Hartshorne, "Whitehead's Idea of God," in *The Philosophy of Alfred North Whitehead* (The Library of Living Philosophers, Vol. III, Northwestern University, Evanston and Chicago : 1941), p. 559, footnote 65.

Whitehead says, "is meant that the status of any eternal object A in this realm is capable of analysis into an indefinite number of subordinate relationships of limited scope. For example if B and C are two other eternal objects, then there is some perfectly definite relationship $R(A,B,C)$ which involves A, B, C only, as to require the mention of no other definite eternal objects in the capacity of relata. Of course, the relationship $R(A,B,C)$ may involve subordinate relationships which are themselves eternal objects, and $R(A,B,C)$ is also itself an eternal object. Also there will be other relationships which in the same sense involve only A, B, C. We have now to examine how, having regard to the internal relatedness of eternal objects, this limited relationship $R(A,B,C)$ is possible.

"The reason for the existence of finite relationships in the realm of eternal objects is that relationships of these objects among themselves are entirely unselective, and are systematically complete. We are discussing possibility; so that every relationship which is possible is thereby in the realm of possibility. Every such relationship of each eternal object is founded upon the perfectly definite status of that object as a relatum in the general scheme of relationships. This definite status is what I have termed the 'relational essence' of the object. This relational essence is determinable by reference to the object alone, and does not require reference to any other objects. ... The meaning of the words 'any' and 'some' springs from this principle — that is to say, the meaning of the 'variable' in logic. ..." [3]

One interpretation of these remarks allows us to envisage the realm of eternal objects in terms of the (simplified) theory of types. Given A, B, and C as eternal objects (of given type) there exist triadic relations R (of appropriate relative type) having A, B, and C as relata (in this order). Any such R itself is an eternal object, relationally contained in or "involving" some triadic relation S also holding among A, B, and C. Further, these various relations are "entirely unselective" and the totality of them is "systematically complete," in the sense that they are all available as objects (values for variables) of appropriate type.

Eternal objects are possibilities in the sense that they may or may not be exemplified in specific instances. A property may or may not "ingress" into some actual occasion and is thus a possible for that

---

[3] *Science and the Modern World*, pp. 236-237. All subsequent quotations are from this work.

occasion. Whitehead seems to use "possible" as a mere *manière de parler*, and all ostensible uses of it seem to be eliminable without loss of content.

Further evidence that Whitehead is tacitly presupposing type theory comes from considering the notion of the *grade* of a complex eternal object. Again Whitehead's own words : "A definite finite relationship [or class] involving the definite eternal objects of a limited set of such objects is itself an eternal object : it is those eternal objects as in that relationship [or class]. I will call such an eternal object 'complex.' The eternal objects which are the relata in [or members of] a complex eternal object will be called the 'components' of that eternal object. Also if any of these relata [or members] are themselves complex, their components will be called 'derivative components' of the original complex object. Also the components of derivative components will also be called derivative components of the original object. Thus the complexity of an eternal object means its analysability into a relationship of component eternal objects. Also the analysis of the general scheme of relatedness of eternal objects means its exhibition as a multiplicity of complex eternal objects. An eternal object, such as a definite shade of green, which cannot be analysed into a relationship of components, will be called 'simple.'

"We can now explain how the analytical character of the realm of eternal objects allows of an analysis of that realm into grades.

"In the lowest grade of eternal objects are to be placed those objects ... [which] ... are simple. This is the grade of zero complexity. Next consider any set of such objects, finite or infinite as to the number of its members. For example, consider the set of three eternal objects A, B, C of which none is complex. Let us write $R(A,B,C)$ [as above] for some definite possible relatedness of A, B, C. To take a simple example, A, B, C may be three definite colours with the spatio-temporal relatedness to each other of three faces of a regular tetrahedron, anywhere at any time. Then $R(A,B,C)$ is another complex object of the lowest complex grade. Analogously there are eternal objects of successively higher grades. In respect to any complex eternal object, $S(D_1,D_2,...,D_n)$, the eternal objects D_1, ... ,D_n, are called the components of $S(D_1,...,D_n)$. It is obvious that the grade of complexity to be ascribed to $S(D_1,...,D_n)$, is to be taken as one above the highest grade of complexity to be found among its components." [4]

[4] Pp. 239-240.

The close formal affinity between the grade of an eternal object and the type of a class or relation in simplified type theory is evident. Presumably the individuals, or entities of lowest or first type, are actual occasions and only such. The simple eternal objects (of zero grade but second type) then comprise the classes of and relations between or among actual occasions. Complex eternal objects of first grade (but third type) are classes of or relations between or among such classes and relations (and perhaps actual occasions also). And so on for all higher types and grades.

Whitehead goes on to note that "as we pass from the grade of simple eternal objects to higher and higher grades of complexity, we are indulging in higher grades of abstraction from the realm of possibility. ... We can now conceive the successive stages of a definite progress toward some assigned mode of abstraction from the realm of possibility, involving a progress (in thought) through successive grades of increasing complexity. I will call any such route of progress 'an abstractive hierarchy.' Any abstractive hierarchy, finite or infinite, is based upon some definite group of simple eternal objects. This group will be called the 'base' of the hierarchy. Thus the base of an abstractive hierarchy is a set of objects of zero complexity." [5]

Whitehead defines formally the notion of being an abstractive hierarchy as follows.

"An 'abstractive hierarchy based upon g,' where g is a group of simple eternal objects, is a set of eternal objects which satisfy the following conditions,

(i) the members of g belong to it, and are the only simple eternal objects in the hierarchy,

(ii) the components of any complex eternal object in the hierarchy are also members of the hierarchy, and

(iii) any set of eternal objects belonging to the hierarchy, whether all of the same grade or whether differing among themselves as to grade, are jointly among the components or derivative components of at least one eternal object which also belongs to the hierarchy [Condition of Connexity].

"It is to be noticed that the components of an eternal object are necessarily of a lower grade of complexity than itself. Accordingly any member of such a hierarchy, which is of the first grade of com-

[5] P. 241.

plexity, can have as components only members of the group *g*; and any member of the second grade can have as components only members of the first grade, and members of *g*; and so on for the higher grades." [6]

Also, "[a]n abstractive hierarchy is called 'finite' if it stops at a finite grade of complexity. It is called 'infinite' if it includes members belonging respectively to all degrees of complexity." [7]

Taken literally, Whitehead's definition of being an abstractive hierarchy cannot be given upon the basis of the theory of types. For this definition variables ranging over objects of more than one type would seem to be needed, an abstractive hierarchy being a set of objects of different logical type. But this does not mean that the definition cannot be reconciled with type theory. Rather we may regard Whitehead's definition as a loose, preliminary, presystematic one, and our task is now to reformulate its essential intent in a more exact way. This can be done by suitable technical devices.

First, let us reflect upon the presystematic definition a little more closely. The clauses (i) and (ii) seem clear enough, at least in a preliminary way. But (iii), the "condition of connexity," is not clear. Perhaps Whitehead intends it to be taken as follows :

(iii)' given any set of eternal objects belonging to the hierarchy, whether all of the same grade or whether differing among themselves as to grade, every member of that set is a component or a derivative component of at least one member of the hierarchy.

But if we take (iii) as (iii)', we note then that there can be no hierarchies of finite grade. Because according to (iii)', given the set of *all* eternal objects in the hierarchy, there will always be one more eternal object having as components or derivative components the members of thet set. Thus that set cannot be finite. So perhaps (iii) should be taken disjunctively along with the following :

(iii)'' there exists at least one eternal object belonging to the hierarchy containing as components all other eternal objects belonging to the hierarchy, whether all of the same grade or whether differing among themselves as to grade.

On the basis of (iii)'' we can have hierarchies of finite grade.

A hierarchy of finite grade has a maximum grade. Whitehead says that "it is characteristic of this grade that a member of it is a compo-

---

[6] Pp. 241-242.
[7] P. 242.

nent of no other eternal object belonging to any grade of the hierarchy. Also it is evident that this grade of maximum complexity must possess only one member; for otherwise the condition of connexity would not be satisfied." [8] This of course follows according to (iii)'', because if there were two eternal objects of maximal grade, there would have to be another of the same grade having the two as components. But, as Whitehead has previously explained, the components of an eternal object must be of lower grade than the eternal object itself. The "sole member of the grade of maximum complexity" is called the "*vertex*."

Tentatively and presystematically, then, let us take (iii) as the disjunction of (iii)' and (iii)'', to provide for hierarchies of both finite and infinite grade.

How now can we give the definition of being an abstractive hierarchy without violating the theory of types? For finite hierarchies, this can be done quite simply. For infinite hierarchies, we must have recourse to *transfinite* types. Little work on the logic of transfinite types had been done at the time Whitehead was writing, and indeed little has been done since. But Whitehead's mathematical imagination may well have led him to envisage such a theory. And surely the use of such a theory does no violence to the spirit of his approach to cosmology.

Now let us attempt to formulate a little more rigorously what seems to be the intent of Whitehead's definition.

First let us give an example of what we shall regard as a finite abstractive hierarchy H based on g. g is a class of simple eternal objects, say A, B, and C. These in turn are presumably properties of actual occasions, which themselves are of type 1. Let R and Q be two different dyadic relations (of type 3) holding among A, B, and C. Suppose that S is a class of eternal objects of which A is a member. Let R and Q stand in some dyadic relation K (of type 4). Finally, let Λ be a septadic relation (of 5th type) holding among K, R, Q, S, A, B, and C. As is customary, let us write '$\{A\}$' to stand for the class

---

[8] P. 243. The condition of connexity for finite hierarchies, seems to have been overlooked by Nathaniel Lawrence, in *Whitehead's Philosophical Development* (University of California Press : Berkeley, 1956), p. 331, footnote 62, where he says that he does not find in the conditions which an abstractive hierarchy must satisfy "anything that forces ... him to the conclusion that there could not be an abstractive hierarchy whose highest grade of complexity might contain several members that did not lend themselves to any further 'synthesis.' "

whose only member is A, '$\{A,B\}$,' for the class whose only members are A and B, and so on. H may then be identified with the class (of type 6)

$$\{A, \{K\}, \{\{R\}\}, \{\{Q\}\}, \{\{S\}\}, \{\{\{A\}\}\}, \{\{\{B\}\}\}, \{\{\{C\}\}\}\}.$$

Note that H is then a homogeneous class, all of its members being of the same logical type, and hence may be accommodated within type theory. The relation A here is the vertex. If we regard finite abstractive hierarchies as homogeneous classes in this way, we surely do no violence to Whitehead's intent.

Note that the vertex of a finite abstractive hierarchy uniquely determines the hierarchy and conversely. Therefore the one can presumably be defined in terms of the other. Let us first define the notion of being a vertex and then the notion of being an abstractive hierarchy. The vertex of course depends upon the class of eternal objects g, just as the abstractive hierarchy does.

We may say that an m-adic relation V_g^m of type n is a *vertex based upon* a non-null class g of eternal objects if and only if:

(1) V_g^m contains at least one relatum of type 2, one of type 3, ... , and one of type n-1,

(2) every member of g is a relatum of V_g^m,

(3) every relatum of V_g^m of type 3 is a class of or relation between or among members of g,

(4) every relatum of V_g^m of type 4 is a class of or a relation between or among relata of V_g^m of type 3,

.

.

.

.

(n-1) every relatum of V_g^m of type n-1 is a class of or a relation between or among relata of V_g^m of type n-2.

The abstractive hierarchy H based on g with vertex V_g^m is, then, a class of type $n+1$ whose members are the following:

(1) V_g^m itself,

(2) given any component β of V_g^m of type 3, the unit class

$$\overbrace{\{\cdots\{\{\beta\}\}\cdots\}}^{n\text{-3 times}\ \ n\text{-3 times}}$$

is a member of H,

(3) given any component β of V_g^m of type 4, the unit class

$$n\text{-4 times } n\text{-4 times}$$
$$\overbrace{\qquad}\overbrace{\qquad}$$
$$\{\cdots\{\{\beta\}\}\cdots\}$$

is a member of H,

$$\cdot$$
$$\cdot$$
$$\cdot$$

(n-2) given any component β of V_g^m of type n-1, the unit class $\{\beta\}$ is a member of H.

These definitions are not intended as rigorously formal ones. For such, a suitable formalization of type theory must be presupposed. And such definitions would take us too deeply into technical matters. But nonetheless, these definitions could easily be formalized. Actually they are *definition-schemata*, each stipulating an infinity of definitions, one for each $n \leq 3$. Note that since the vertex V_g^m is an m-adic relation, m must be $\leq n$-1, because the vertex has as arguments at least one class or relation of type n-1, one of type n-2, and so on. But it may have as arguments more than one class or relation of these types.

To extend these definitions to hierarchies of infinite grade would presumably be to employ transfinite types, as has already been suggested.

"It is to be noted," Whitehead says,[9] "that the base [g] of an abstractive hierarchy may contain any number of members, finite or infinite. Further, the infinity of the number of members has nothing to do with the question as to whether the hierarchy be finite of infinite" (i.e., whether the hierarchy be of finite or infinite grade). We must not construe "has nothing to do with" here too literally. Because if g is infinite, how then can we form a vertex V_g^m for finite n? The vertex would have to have as relata each of this infinity of members of g.[10] But there exist presumably only relations of finite degree. Therefore if g is infinite, an abstractive hierarchy based upon g cannot be of finite grade. On the other hand, g may be finite and yet there are abstractive hierarchies based on g of infinite grade.

Suppose g contains just m members, and let V_g^m be the vertex of

[9] P. 243.
[10] It seems doubtful, but not impossible, that Whitehead has in mind here relations of infinite degree.

some abstractive hierarchy based on g. Consider now any relations of type 3 which are relata of V_g^m. None of these relations need be of degree $> m$, because any relation holding among all these m eternal objects may be regarded as an n-adic relation.[11] But there is no limit to the number of such relations, except that it must be at most finite. Suppose in fact there are just k such relations (including classes). Then at the fourth type, there need be no relations of degree $< m + k$, for similar reasons. And similarly at each type $< n$.

"In any actual occasion α," Whitehead says, "there will be a group g of simple eternal objects which are ingredient in that group [does Whitehead not mean rather : which are ingredient in α?] in the most concrete mode. This complete ingredience in an occasion ... is evidently of its own kind and cannot be defined in terms of anything else. But it has a peculiar characteristic which necessarily attaches to it. This characteristic is that there is an *infinite* abstractive hierarchy based upon g which is such that all its members are equally involved in this complete inclusion [ingression] in α.

"The existence of such an infinite abstractive hierarchy is what is meant by the statement that it is impossible to complete the description of an actual occasion by means of concepts. I will call this infinite abstractive hierarchy which is associated with α 'the associated hierarchy of α' ... [E]vidently in describing an actual occasion α," he goes on, "we are nearer to the total concrete fact when we describe α by predicating of it some member of its associated hierarchy, which is of a high grade of complexity. We have then said more about α. Thus, with a high grade of complexity we gain in approach to the full concreteness of α, and with a low grade we lose in this approach. Accordingly the simple eternal objects represent the extreme of abstraction from an actual occasion; whereas simple eternal objects represent the minimum of abstraction from the realm of possibility."[12]

Of course Whitehead is using the word "predicating" here only in a somewhat Pickwickian sense. Suppose g is $\{A,B,C\}$ and that 'A', 'B', and 'C' may be predicated of an actual occasion α. Let '$R(A,B,C)$' hold and let R be a "member" of the infinite associated hierarchy of α. Then 'R' may also presumably be "predicated" of α, and also the relation R is then ingredient in α. And similarly for any other relation or class in the associated hierarchy.

---

[11] E.g., '$R(A,B,A)$' may be written as '$S(A,B)$' for a suitable S.
[12] Pp. 244-246.

The main features of the doctrine of abstractive hierarchies have now been indicated, and we have tried to show how it is consonant with type theory. "The meaning of the words 'any' and 'some' springs from this principle — that is to say, the meaning of the 'variable' in logic," Whitehead points out.[13] The use of 'any' and 'some' are therefore presumably to be construed throughout in accord with type theory, probably the only logic Whitehead knew. Further, he had little interest in alternative logics. "One God, one country, one logic," he is said to have exclaimed upon first learning of the Tarski-Lukasiewicz three-valued logics.

[13] P. 237.

VI

STEPS TOWARDS A PRAGMATIC PROTOGEOMETRY

"Bene speremus, hominum enim vestigia video."

1

Mathematics is not a subject removed from metaphysical toil, but part and parcel of the system of our knowledge and of the sciences as a whole. It would be a truly extraordinary situation in the cosmos if it were otherwise. If it were, there would be straightaway a bifurcation to be explained. An adequate account of knowledge without a bifurcation is difficult enough, and next to impossible with one. Further, there seem to be no well-grounded reasons why mathematics should be thought to constitute one kind of knowledge and the other sciences another. What precisely is the difference here anyhow? Is it fundamental? And why should there be this difference? Not that there are not distinctions, of course. There always are between or among the sciences, but these should not, it would seem, be regarded as fundamental distinctions of kind. In any case, it is of interest to try to view mathematics as part of an integrated and comprehensive system rather than as someting special or *sui generis.*

By 'mathematics' is meant here primarily arithmetic and geometry, together of course with whatever can be constructed in terms of these. And by 'arithmetic' one means that of the positive integers, perhaps including 0 (in which case we speak of the natural numbers). By 'geometry' is meant primarily here what is called 'protogeometry', which includes only notions and principles of a very basic kind enunciated before getting on too far into the specialized geometries, Euclidean, Reimannian, and so on, of a higher number of dimensions.

The term 'protogeometry' is adapted from Paul Lorenzen [1] — the

---

[1] In his *Normative Logic and Ethics* (Bibliographisches Institut, Mannheim-Zürich : 1969), p. 60.

term, note, but not the content — who speaks of *geometry, chronometry,* and *hylometry* as constituting the three branches of what he calls 'protophysics'. According to him, these three "are a-priori theories which make empirical measurement of space, time, and materia [material bodies] "possible." They have to be established before physics in the modern sense of an empirical science, with its hypothetical fields of forces, can begin." Of course physics can "begin" any way it wishes and physicists are free to proceed howsoever they best see fit. The point of protophysics is that it provides a "rational reconstruction" or "logical map" of what the physicist presupposes. Fundamental here are the integers as used in counting and measurement (with the principles of arithmetic), and of course geometric elements (with at least rudimentary principles governing them). Lorenzen's own characterization of protophysics is unsatisfactory for a variety of reasons.[2] It seems best then to begin on a somewhat new footing provided by event logic, about which more will be said in a moment.

2

The *sui generis* approach to mathematics is via set theory. Many alternative set theories are currently on the market clamoring for buyers. It is not clear that any of them are fully satisfactory, however, even in the eyes of their proponents. There is little agreement as to which are preferable, on purely cognitive grounds, and the proponents of any one are eloquent in proclaiming its special virtues. Opponents are equally eloquent in pointing out the *ad hoc* and artificial character of crucial axioms needed to protect the system from the well known paradoxes. Even with this artificiality, convincing proofs of consistency are not easy to achieve, and it may well be maintained that none has been, or perhaps ever will be, forthcoming in acceptable terms.

Why then bother about set theory at all? one may ask. To provide a foundation for mathematics, one could answer. Whether mathematics is in any genuine sense founded upon set theory, however, may be doubted. Mathematics is something quite different, it may be maintained, more constructivistic, more intuitionistic, more numerical, more

---

[2] See the author's "Truth and Its Illicit Surrogates," *Neue Hefte für Philosophie,* forthcoming, and "On Lorenzen's *Normative Logic and Ethics,*" in *Events, Reference, and Logical Form.*

intimately linked with the other sciences and concerned with supplying suitable methods and procedures to them. If mathematics is so viewed, the set-theoretic approach to its foundations is not appropriate.

It has been maintained that set theory is needed only in mathematics, not outside it. According to Father Bocheński, it "seems that ... [higher level] functors and quantifiers occur *only* in formal sciences, and are not needed in [the] empirical sciences."[3] Outside mathematics, the theory of *virtual* classes and relations seems always to suffice wherever classes or sets are needed at all.

It is usually thought that sets are essential in semantics, being presupposed fundamentally in Tarski's celebrated definition of the truth concept. Simpler methods are known, however, for providing for truth foregoing such powerful devices. And similarly for syntax and pragmatics. Hence there is no need for set theory as a foundation for the theory of truth and other areas of semiotic.

If one is sensitive to matters of ontic commitment, one may well be bothered by the ontic status of sets and allied objects.[4] Any use of them commits one to a vast realm of "abstract" objects of dubious character. Such commitment is not altogether welcome on philosophical grounds and is to be circumvented if possible. In any case it raises an undesirable problem that can otherwise be avoided. As good a maxim as any in philosophy is that *problems should not be multiplied beyond necessity*.

Some think that set-theoretic methods are indispensable in the study of the "deep structure" of natural language. The so-called model-theoretic semantics of "possible worlds," under current exploration and favored by many, presupposes set theory in most fundamental ways. It is far from clear, however, that such semantics succeeds where simpler methods fail. The study of deep structure from a logico-semantical point of view is still in its infancy, and all manner of different approaches to it should surely be explored. In the long run, simpler methods usually carry the day over complicated ones, however, in the sciences as elsewhere. There is thus little reason to think that the new linguistics, when it comes to terms with modern logic, will provide any exception to this.

[3] See his *The Problem of Universals*, with A. Church and N. Goodman (University of Notre Dame Press, Notre Dame: 1956), p. 42.

[4] See especially W. V. Quine, *Word and Object* (The Technology Press of Massachusetts Institute of Technology and John Wiley and Sons, New York and London : 1960), pp. 119 f. and 241 ff., and *Belief, Existence, and Meaning*, Chapter II.

Still another argument against set theory will be presented below, in terms of *extrapolation*. The natural numbers and the basic geometric entities emerge naturally by extrapolation from familiar entities and experiences, it will be maintained. Classes and sets cannot arise in such fashion, it seems, being *sui generis*. One has to make a tremendous mental leap to grasp them. They do not seem to arise in the system of our knowledge along with the rest of what we know, but must instead occupy a very special place. This need for special handling in precisely what is denied in the account of arithmetic and geometry to be given.

3

The positive integers have been with us for some centuries now, holding their little heads as proudly as can be. God is supposed to have made them, according to Kronecker, and all the rest of mathematics is the work of man. The view here, however, is that even the integers are human artifacts.

The form

$$\text{'} e_1 \text{ Crrlt } e_2,e_3,F \text{'}$$

has been introduced elsewhere to express that person e_1 correlates a string of stroke-marks "'||||'..." with those parts of the object e_3 that are in the virtual class F.[5] Thus where the e_2 is a single mark, either e_3 would itself be in F or would contain one and only one part that is in F. Where e_2 consists of just two strokes, e_3 would not be in F but would contain exactly two distinct proper parts that are. And so on. In this way a theory of counting is developed that serves as a basis for arithmetic. Expressions for the integers are defined in appropriate contexts, and the principles of arithmetic proved on suitable assumptions.

Arithmetic thus arises out of event logic in a natural way by extrapolation and without the use of any new type of objects as values for variables. On this basis the theory of rational numbers, positive and negative, may be developed in familiar fashion, as well as a constructivistic theory of the real numbers. Whether anything more is really ever required in applications of mathematics in the sciences is a moot point. In any case, a very considerable portion of standard numerical mathematics may be accommodated on the kind of basis described.

[5] See "The Pragmatics of Counting," in *Events, Reference, and Logical Form.*

4

Geometry like arithmetic is a product of human ingenuity. There are no geometrical entities "out there" waiting to be discovered. There are no eternal geometric truths independent of us awaiting formulation. On the contrary, it is *we* who construct the geometric entities in just such fashion as we please, doing so to serve some suitable human or noetic purpose. It is we who formulate geometric principles, in many alternative ways, adjusting them into total patterns of interest on their own account and often useful in practice. By a 'pattern' here one means what is usually called 'an axiom system'. The pattern incorporates implicitly the basic principles determinative of the particular kind of geometry.

If protogeometry like arithmetic is a branch of pragmatics, we must search for suitable basic pragmatical primitives in terms of which it may be expressed.

Geometry of the basic kinds postulates that there are such things as points, lines, planes, and so on, interrelated in various ways. For the moment let us consider only points. According to Euclid, in the very first definition of Book I of the *Elements*, "A point is that which has no parts, or which has no magnitude." By 'parts' here of course is meant 'proper parts'. Although Euclid fails to enunciate it, clearly there are assumed to be such things as points. Non-Euclidean systems make such an assumption also. If geometry is regarded as a part of a wider scheme, a good deal more needs to be said as to what points are and how they are arrived at. And a good deal more needs to be said as to whether there are such entities. *As a matter of fact there are no points*, according to the theory to be put forward here, and that ends the matter. As convenient, idealized fictions, however, arrived at by extrapolation from what there actually is, they may be introduced and accommodated in suitable linguistic contexts. Just as there are no integers but merely strings of marks and suitable acts of correlation, so there are no points but merely certain pseudo-objects arrived at by suitable *Gedankenexperimente* or acts of extrapolation.

In event logic there are such things as *point events* and there may be such a thing as a *null* event, as already remarked. Let 'e_1 P e_2' express as above that event e_1 is a *part* of event e_2. That e_1 is a *proper part* of e_2 may be expressed by 'e_1 PP e_2'. Clearly

$$(e_1)(e_2)(e_1 \text{ PP } e_2 \equiv (e_1 \text{ P } e_2 \cdot \sim e_2 \text{ P } e_1)).$$

Let 'Null e' express that the event e is null. Then

$\quad$ (Ee)Null e,

$\quad$ (e_1)(e_2)((Null e_1 $\cdot$ Null e_2) $\supset$ $e_1 = e_2$),

$\quad$ (e)(Null $e \equiv \sim$ (Ee_1)($\sim$ Null e_1 $\cdot$ e_1 P e)),

$\quad$ (e)(Null $e \equiv \sim$ (Ee_1)e_1 PP e),

and

$\quad$ (e)(Null $e \equiv$ (e_1)e P e_1).

There is such a thing as a null event, there is at most one null event, every null event is such that it has no part other than a null event, every null event has no proper part and conversely, and every null event is a part of every event and conversely.

Point events are non-null actual events having no proper parts other than the null event. Thus

'PtEv e' may abbreviate '($\sim$ Null e $\cdot$ (e_1)((e_1 P e $\cdot$ $\sim$ Null e_1) $\supset$ e P e_1))'.

It seems reasonable in event logic to postulate that there are point events and to regard them as the most basic kind of non-null entity available. They are very like the little atomic triangles of Plato's *Timaeus* and the actual entities, the "merest puffs of experience," of Whitehead's *Process and Reality*.

5

It might be thought that protogeometric points could be identified outright with point events, but this would not do. Point events have a little magnitude, to speak loosely, whereas points have none. Point events can be summed into larger objects, every non-null event being the *fusion* — in the sense of the calculus of individuals — of the virtual class of point events that are parts of it.

$\quad$ (e)($\sim$ Null $e \supset e =$ Fu'$\{e' \ni$ (PtEv e' $\cdot$ e'P e)$\}$).[6]

Protogeometric points likewise can be summed, the result, however, having no more magnitude than the summands. Further, the cardinality of the PtEv's is less than that of the protogeometric points. The latter is non-denumerable, the former at most denumerable, perhaps even finite.

Further kinds of pragmatic correlation relations may now be introduced in context to supplement (1) above, in particular now

---

[6] Note that $\{e_3\text{--}e\text{--}\}$ here is a virtual class, whereas $\hat{e}(\text{--}e\text{--})$ would be a *real* one in the sense of being a value for a variable.

(2)   'e_1 Crrltp$_t$ e_2,e_3'.

This is to express that person e_1 correlates the event e_2 (regarded as a "point") with the PtEv e_3 as the "parent entity." Where 'Per e_1' expresses that e_1 is a person, clearly

$(e_1)(e_2)(e_3)(e_1$ Crrltp$_t$ $e_2,e_3 \supset$ (Per e_1 · PtEv e_3)).

Let 'e_1 Acpt e_2' express that e_1 accepts the sentence e_2 of L, and let 'e_1 Ref e_2,e_2' express that e_1 uses the sign event e_2 to refer to e_3. Then (D1) 'e_1 Crrltp$_t$ e_2,e_3' may abbreviate '(Per e_1 · PtEv e_3 · (Ee') $(Ee'')(Ee_4)(e_1$ Ref e',e_2 · e_1 Ref e'', e_3 · e_1 Acpt e_4 · $\Gamma e_4))$', where 'Γe_4' expresses that e_4 is an inscription of the shape '(' followed by e' followed by 'PP' followed by e'' followed by '.' followed by '$\sim$ $(Ee_5)e_5$ PP' followed by e' followed by ')'. (This clause merely spells out the structural description of the shape of the sentence that person e_1 accepts.[7])

Although this definition looks somewhat laborious, actually it is quite simple. It defines (2) above as holding when person e_1 accepts a sentence to the effect that the entity or "point" e_2 is a proper part of point event e_3 but itself has no proper part. By accepting such a sentence e_1 is deliberately propogating a fiction. He is "imagining" a situation that might obtain. He takes or regards the entity e_2 here as an imagined point.

What is a point then? Let

(D2) 'Pt$_e$' e' abbreviate '$(Ee_1)e'$ Crrltp$_t$ e,e_1',

so that a point is merely an entity imagined or accepted by someone to be a proper part of some PtEv but having no proper part itself.

(D2) might strike one as providing a very strange conception of a point. It puts points, and therewith geometry, under a propositional attitude, so to speak. Further, all points deliberately become fictionalized. Still, there are such points if there are geometers to entertain them. In fact there are as many such points as any geometer cares to entertain. And although the sentence e_4 of (D1) is false, it may be true that the geometer entertains it. Thus true sentences of geometry may be formulated even though the sentence under the propositional attitude is false.

The notion of a point has some kinship with Whitehead's notion of a coordinate division, a fundamental notion of his theory of extensive connection. This notion was discussed in IV above.

---

[7] On structural descriptions within inscriptional semantics, see *Truth and Denotation*, p. 247.

6

Suppose now that the foregoing, or something like it, gives a reasonable notion of a point. How do we go on to lines, planes, and so on?

Another kind of correlation may now be introduced, this time as a primitive. Let

(3)   'e Crrlt$_{Bet}$ e_1,e_2,e_3'

express primitively that person e correlates some point of PtEv e_1 with some point of PtEv e_3 to form a line segment between them with some point of PtEv e_2 lying between these two points.

Let now, to simplify notation,

'$\sim e_5 =_e e_5$' be short for '$(Ee_2)(Ee_3)(Ee')(e$ Ref $e_2,e_4 \cdot e$ Ref $e_3,e_5 \cdot \Gamma e' \cdot e$ Acpt $e')$',

where '$\Gamma e'$' expresses that e' is an inscription consisting of a '$\sim$' followed by the sign event e_2 followed by an '$=$' followed by e_3. And similarly for other forms of sentence. Further, to remind us that it is always a geometer, or at least *homo quā geometres*, who is the person involved, let 'g' (or 'g') be used throughout in place of 'e' as the relevant parameter.

Immediately then it is to hold that

$(g)(e_1)(e_2)(e_3)(g$ Crrlt$_{Bet}$ $e_1,e_2,e_3 \supset$ (Per $g \cdot$ PtEv $e_1 \cdot$ PtEv $e_2 \cdot$ PtEv $e_3 \cdot (Ee_4)(Ee_5)(Ee_6)(g$ Crrlt$_{Pt}$ $e_4,e_1 \cdot g$ Crrlt$_{Pt}$ $e_5,e_2 \cdot g$ Crrlt$_{Pt}$ $e_6,e_3 \cdot \sim e_4 =_g e_5 \cdot \sim e_5 =_g e_6 \cdot \sim e_6 =_g e_4)))$,

$(g)(e_1)(e_2)(e_3)(g$ Crrlt$_{Bet}$ $e_1,e_2,e_3 \supset g$ Crrlt$_{Bet}$ $e_3,e_2,e_1)$.

Let

'e Seg$_g$ e_1,e_2' abbreviate '$(Pt_g$ $e_1 \cdot Pt_g$ $e_2 \cdot \sim e_1 =_g e_2 \cdot (e')(Pt_g$ $e' \supset (e'$ PP$_g$ $e \equiv (e' =_g e_1$ v $e' =_g e_2$ v $(Ee_3)(Ee_4)(Ee_5)(g$ Crrlt$_{Bet}$ $e_3, e_4,e_5 \cdot g$ Crrlt$_{Pt}$ $e_1,e_3 \cdot g$ Crrlt $e_2,e_4 \cdot g$ Crrlt$_{Pt}$ $e',e_5)))))$'.

The definiendum expresses that g takes e as a line *segment* with e_1 and e_2 as endpoints. Then also

$(g)(e_1)(e_2)(e_3)(g$ Crrlt$_{Bet}$ $e_1,e_2,e_3 \supset (Ee)((Ee_4)(Ee_5)(Ee_6)(g$ Crrlt$_{Pt}$ $e_4,e_1 \cdot g$ Crrlt$_{Pt}$ $e_5,e_2 \cdot g$ Crrlt$_{Pt}$ $e_6,e_3 \cdot e$ Seg$_g$ $e_4,e_6 \cdot e_4$ PP$_g$ $e \cdot e_5$ PP$_g$ $e \cdot e_6$ PP$_g$ $e))$.

These three principles express familiar laws, that if a point b is between a and c, then a, b, and c are distinct points on a line segment and b is also between c and a.

Note that it is not required, where g Crrlt$_{Bet}$ e_1,e_2,e_3, that the PtEv's e_1, e_2, and e_3 are distinct. They may or may not be. The correlated points, however, must be.

Note also that where e Seg$_g$ e_1,e_2, only the existence of e is required, not necessarily uniqueness.

What now is a line? Let

'e L$_g$ e_1,e_2' abbreviate '(Pt$_g$ e_1 · Pt$_g$ e_2 · ∼ e_1 =$_g$ e_2 · $(e')((Ee_3)(Ee_4)e'$ Seg$_g$ e_3,e_4 ⊃ $(e'$ PP$_g$ e ≡ $(Ee_3)(Ee_4)(Ee_5)(Ee_6)(e'$ Seg$_g$ e_1,e_3 · g Crrlt$_{Pt}$ e_1,e_4 · g Crrlt$_{Pt}$ e_2,e_5 · g Crrlt$_{Pt}$ e_3,e_6 · (g Crrlt$_{Bet}$ e_1,e_3,e_2 v g Crrlt$_{Bet}$ e_1,e_3,e_2)))))'

A line determined by points correlated with e_1 and e_2, according to this definition, is taken to consist of all segments determined by points correlated with e_1 to e_3, so to speak, where the point correlated with e_2 is taken to be between the points correlated with e_1 and e_3 or the point correlated with e_1 is taken to be between these correlated with e_3 and e_2.

The foregoing principle may now be strengthened to read :

$(g)(e_1)(e_2)(e_3)(g$ Crrlt$_{Bet}$ e_1,e_2,e_3 ⊃ $(Ee)(Ee_4)(Ee_4)(Ee_4)(g$ Crrlt$_{Pt}$ e_4,e_1 · g Crrlt$_{Pt}$ e_5,e_2 · g Crrlt$_{Pt}$ e_6,e_3 · e L$_g$ e_4,e_6 · e_4 PP$_g$ e · e_5 PP$_g$ e · e_6 PP$_g$ e)).

This states in effect that if a point b is between a and c, then a, b, and c all fall on a line.

Two lines intersect each other if they have a point in common. Thus

'e_1 Intsct$_g$ e_2' abbreviates '$(Ee_3)(Ee_4)(Ee_5)(Ee_6)(Ee)$(Pt$_g$ e · e_1 L$_g$ e_3,e_4 · e_2 L$_g$ e_5,e_6 · e P$_g$ e_1 · e P$_g$ e_2)'.

What now is a plane as determined by three non-colinear points? It may be taken as consisting of the three lines determined by these three points together with all lines that intersect them. Thus

'e Plg e_1,e_2,e_3' may abbreviate '(Pt$_g$ e_1 · Pt$_g$ e_2 · Pt$_g$ e_3 · ∼ e_1 =$_g$ e_2 · ∼ e_2 =$_g$ e_3 · ∼ e_1 =$_g$ e_3 · ∼ $(Ee_4)(Ee_5)(Ee_6)(e_4$ L$_g$ e_6,e_6 · e_1 PP$_g$ e_4 · e_2 PP$_g$ e_4 · e_3 PP$_g$ e_4) · $(Ee_4)(Ee_5)(Ee_6)(e_4$ L$_g$ e_1,e_2 · e_5 L$_g$ e_2,e_3 · e_6 L$_g$ e_1,e_3 · $(e')((Ee_7)(Ee_8)e'$ L$_g$ e_7,e_8 ⊃ $(e'$ PP$_g$ e ≡ $(e'$ =$_g$ e_4 v e' =$_g$ e_5 v e' =$_g$ e_6 v $(Ee_7)(Ee_8)(e'$ L$_g$ e_7,e_8 · $(e'$ Intsct$_g$ e_4 v e' Intsct$_g$ e_5 v e' Intsct$_g$ e_6)))))))'.

Clearly suitable principles may now be laid down interrelating these various notions as needed for special purposes.

7

The foregoing material may no doubt be improved upon in various ways as to detail, but enough has been shown surely to enable us to see how protogeometry is supposed to emerge from event logic, on the one hand, and lead on to the development of geometry proper, on the other. Some of the principles given might be suitable to take as axioms. They are akin in fact to some of Hilbert's axioms for Euclidean geometry.[8] However, nothing like a complete axiomatization is attempted here. In fact, an axiomatization would belong to geometry itself rather than to protogeometry. Protogeometry is concerned merely with the forms of expression allowed, the vocabulary, and with how this vocabulary may be accommodated in the underlying event logic. Protogeometry thus should help us to understand what geometry is and how it relates to other areas of our knowledge. It shows us that geometry is not a subject apart, not "pure," but always within the actual world we inhabit. It shows us that geometry develops always under a propositional attitude and seeks to make explicit what this attitude is. A geometry is a total *Gedankenexperiment*, nothing less, nothing more.

Hilbert's axioms, it will be recalled, divide into five parts : axioms of connection, axioms of order, the axiom of parallels, axioms of congruence, and the axiom of continuity (or the Archimedean axiom). Axioms of the first three kinds may readily be stated within protogeometry in the vocabulary given. These would determine affine geometry, a Euclidean geometry without congruence and without a metric. (There are of course alternatives to the axiom of parallels that may be taken if the purpose at hand warrants — an understatement indeed!) The problem of how best to introduce a metric here is of course the problem of how to introduce methods of measurement in terms of correlational acts. Measurement is in fact merely one more species of correlation. Numbers have been introduced in "The Pragmatics of Counting" only in contexts of counting. Measurement is a more refined species of counting, of lengths, of mass, of force, and so on. In any case, congruence should be readily definable once suitable rules for measurement have been given. The remainder of Hilbert's axioms could then be formulated.

Note that the only specifically geometric primitive required in the above is 'Crrlt$_{Bet}$'. It might seem a defect that such a primitive is required. Somehow it ought to be definable, it would seem, in terms already available. The relation Crrlt$_{Bet}$ involves a notion of betweenness and hence of order, however, and it is not clear how such a notion can be achieved otherwise than by means of adopting a primitive.

---

[8] D. Hilbert, *The Foundations of Geometry*, 3rd ed. (Open Court Publishing Co., LaSalle, Ill. : 1938).

If a temporal topology were assumed, it might be possible to define 'Crrlt$_{Bet}$' in its terms. This however, is a matter beyond the confines of the present discussion.

The methods of protogeometry proceed by extrapolation, as already mentioned above. In other words, the values for variables are just those of the underlying event logic with no additions. The extrapolations occur only under a propositional attitude. The interesting circumstance for the philosophy of geometry is that everything we wish to say is said under the attitude. There are no real points, lines, planes, and so on, but they may be talked about as imagined or fictitious or "theoretical" entities or constructs. Further, as the definition of 'Pt' shows, these constructs can be given in most natural ways just as though they were values for variables.

The question arises as to whether such extrapolation could also be made to work for the theoretical constructs of physics and other sciences. If so, protogeometry would become a branch of protophysics. There is also kinship with instrumentalism. The instrumentalist view of scientific methodology has emphasized all along that theoretical principles and entities are not to be taken at face value anyhow, but are mere devices for giving explanations and predictions in terms of observed data.[9] In putting the theoretical principles and entities under a propositional attitude, a view akin to the instrumentalist one can perhaps be made more precise and explicit.

The only propostional attitude considered is that of acceptance, taken in the sense of provisional acceptation subject to improvement and correction. Is not this the attitude of the scientist anyhow to theoretical entities and principles? No finality of acceptance is required, no belief even, no knowledge — just the attitude of : let us assume them and see how they work out and improve and correct them as needed as we go along.

It was mentioned above that the method of extrapolation would not extend to set theory. The reason is that sets and allied entities are of an altogether new kind. Numbers, points, and so on, can be characterized in terms of the entities already available as values for variables, even if only under the attitude of acceptance. Sets, relations, and other such objects, it seems, must be handled rather as *values for a new kind of variable*. No other methods for formulating set

---

[9] Cf. E. Nagel, *The Structure of Science* (Harcourt, Brace and World, New York : 1961), Chapters 4, 5, and 6.

theory have been developed, and may not even be possible. Further, a protogeometric point is in a real sense "interior" to its parent point event. Whatever a set is, however — and it is to be feared that no one has ever told us — it is "external" to its members. Perhaps all theoretical entities should be regarded as interior to the concrete entities from which they arise by extrapolation, at least microcosmic ones. In any case, it is by no means clear that a set theory could ever be formulated extrapolationally. If not, we have here one more telling argument against such theories.

It was mentioned above that protogeometry is concerned with fundamental notions and principles enunciated before getting too far into the special kinds of geometry. On the other hand, the foregoing has been modelled primarily on Euclidean geometry of three dimensions, as in Hilbert's axiomatization. Strictly there are two stages in the development of protogeometry to be distinguished, those required say, for geometries of Euclidean, Riemannian, Lobatschewskian, or other types, on the one hand, and then notions and principles common to all of these, on the other. The latter can be arrived at only after some delineation of the former.

Strictly protogeometry should consist only of notions neutral as among the specialized geometries and thus of principles common to them. The axioms of the special geometries then can be characterized as certain patterns, in effect, patterns of acceptance, made for certain purposes. A specialized geometry is thus something like a suit of clothes, to be put on or taken off as best befits the occasion. The garments, however, must all be made out of the same basic materials, modelled in high fashion or low as the style demands.

Let '$\Gamma_G\, g,e$' express that e is an inscription consisting of the conjunction of the axioms taken by g as constituting some geometry G. Scientific laws in sciences requiring this type of geometry become then of the form

$$\text{'}(e)(\Gamma_G g,e \supset \text{-----})\text{'},$$

where '-----' presupposes explicitly or implicitly principles of this type of geometry. That scientific laws can be expressed in such forms would be a fundamental tenet of instrumentalism as conceived here. The axioms of G are taken merely as hypotheses where needed, but are not regarded as true. They are merely accepted by the scientist g to perform the tasks he requires of them.

A kind of instrumentalism and constructivistic protogeometry can thus be made to go hand in hand. Hopefully the foregoing provides some useful steps, however tentative and inadequate, as a basis for further exploration and development in order to deepen our understanding of both. *Quod erat faciendum.*

VII

ON MATHEMATICS AND THE GOOD

"Verus philosophus est amator dei et mathematicae."

1

At several places Fitch has put forward a notion of God that deserves more attention than it has received.[1] His notion is subtle; the theory in which it is couched is profound and well organized; and the arguments presented in favor of both the theory and notion are ingenious, original, and not easy to gainsay in its own terms. Nonetheless, both the notion and the theory seem unacceptable for many reasons, some of which have been discussed elsewere.[2] This is not the occasion to repeat or to amplify, so much as to put forward what appears to be a more acceptable alternative.

According to Whitehead, Fitch's mentor to some extent, the "primordial nature of God" is "the unconditioned conceptual valuation of the entire multiplicity of eternal objects." "Perfect" conceptual valuations then are presumably those that accord with the primordial ones. In addition to the primordial nature, the *png*, there is the "consequent nature of God," the *cng*, consisting of all that ever was, is, or shall be. The whole physical cosmos is included in it in a certain way. The full nature of God consists then of the *png* and the *cng* as fused into an indissoluble unity, in fact, as

$$(png \cup cng),$$

as noted in II and III above.

Let us explore now the doctrine of perfection, and of "the revolts of destructive evil, purely self-regarding," that emerge from the Whiteheadian theory of God's di-polor nature. Notions of perfection

---

[1] In particular see F. B. Fitch, "On God and Immortality," *Philosophy and Phenomenological Research* 8 (1948) : 688-693 and "The Perfection of Perfection," *The Monist* 47 (1963) : 466-471.

[2] See "On Fitch's Propositions and States of Affairs."

have fascinated men's minds for millenia and have been of almost perennial interest in philosophical theology. Fitch is one of the first to have used the resources of the new logic to explore one of them. But the Whiteheadian variant, with its attendant notion of evil, is more pliable for theology and has not yet been explored logistically in the Fitchian manner, other than in I and III above.

2

Let us consider now a little more closely than in III above the notion of a "perfect" valuation as one that accords with the primordial nature. Recall the definition of '$e \in$ PerfVal' from § 6 there. In accord with it, a valuation is perfect when its "subject" prehends an EO (with respect to given AO's) to precisely the degree to which that EO is prehended in the primordial nature (with respect to those AO's). And similarly a perfect subjective aim is one in accord with the primordial valuation, as noted in the definition of § 6 of III. A subjective aim of e is perfect when e prehends an EO with respect to given AO's precisely to the degree with which that EO is prehended primordially with respect to those AO's. In a particular instance, of course, e itself may be among those AO's, such an instance being one of self-regard. Each AO as it comes into existence or concrescence has as its "initial" subjective aims only perfect ones. In its initial phase its vision is unclouded, in the sense of having perfection itself constituting its whole teleology. But "destructive evil" soon sets in.

Suppose that i is the degree of the primordial valuation e' with respect to α, e_1, ..., e_m, that is, where

$$\langle e', \text{Prhd}^i, \alpha, e_1, ..., e_m \rangle e'.$$

And let j be the degree of some e's conceptual prehension e'' of α with respect to e_1, ..., e_m, that is, where

$$\langle e, \text{Prhd}^j, \alpha, e_1, ..., e_m \rangle e''.$$

The measure j may be equal to i, or $j < i$, or $j > i$. If $j = i$, there is perfect accord with the primordial valuation. But if $j < i$ or $j > i$, the absolute value $|j - i|$ may be taken as the measure of *disaccord* of e'' with respect to the primordial valuation. The measure of disaccord is also the measure of imperfection of e'', as well as the degree of evil, not actual evil but valuational evil. For the moment we are considering only valuational evil, not the evil of fact or circumstance the may result from disaccord. As a matter of historical fact, $|j - i|$

is almost always > 0, so pervasive is imperfect valuation in the actual world.

Suppose i is as above and that α Ing $e_1,...,e_m$. Suppose further that i has the maximal value 1. Then clearly any state or occasion or circumstance e such that $\langle\alpha,e_1,...,e_m\rangle e$ is therewith perfect, being wholly in accord with the primordial valuation. Such e's are rare enough. And again, any e such that $\langle\alpha,e_1,...,e_m\rangle e$ that is not perfect, is (in a weak sense anyhow) therewith evil. The result is of course that there is evil, evil everywhere, and all of it overwhelming us at every turn.

Are there other modes of perfection and of evil than these two basic ones? It seems not. Of course, there are subdivisions within the two modes. The set of actually evil e's may be partitioned in many interesting ways, evils of omission, of commission, societal, and so on. The reasons for such evil are often very complex. And for valuational evils also. No matter what the reasons are, however, the fact remains that in evil there is violation of the primordial will, urge, or desire that such and such be the case. 'Thy will be done' is a petition that the primordial valuations be realized in practice, on earth and in history as in the *png*.

3

Not all prehensional acts or states of self-love, self-regard, or self-seeking are evil, for some may accord with the primordial nature. Thus if e is a primordial valuation such that $\langle e,\text{Prhd}^1,\alpha,e_1\rangle e$ and e_1 Prhd^1 α,e_1 then any e' such that $\langle\alpha,e_1\rangle e'$ is therewith perfect. And similarly for relational EO's. Suitable self-seeking is thus properly grounded cosmologically. However, such self-seekings are comparatively rare, and most are those that do not accord with the primordial nature. Most self-seekings are thus evil. Cosmologically regarded, the matter is thus rather simple : we should have "suitable" self-regard and not otherwise. Our seekings, both self- and other-directed, should accord with the primordial valuations concerning us, and all other kinds of seekings should be avoided. The very meaning of 'should' is thus firmly established primordially. (There is no "naturalistic fallacy" involved here. The exact determination of what should be is wholly given in the primordial valuations.)

What holds for the moral order obtains for the aesthetic one *mutatis mutandis*. "All order is ... aesthetic order, and the moral order is merely certain aspects of aesthetic order. The actual order is the outcome of the aesthetic order, and the aesthetic order is derived from the immanence of God."[3] The aesthetic order may perhaps be regarded as just that of the primordial valuations. The very notion of order can be regarded as just the set of all ordered $(n + 2)$-tuples μ such that μ has as its factors the relevant elements of a primordial valuation — under 'relevant' including the degree, the EO, and the AO's taken as arguments of that EO, Thus, more specifically, the "aesthetic order" may be regarded merely as the set

$\hat{\mu}(\mathrm{E}i)(\mathrm{E}\alpha)(\mathrm{E}e_1)...(\mathrm{E}e_k)((\mu = \langle i,\alpha,e_1 \rangle \cdot (\mathrm{E}e)(e \,\epsilon\, \mathrm{Val} \cdot 0 \leqq i \leqq 1 \cdot \langle e,\mathrm{Prhd}^i,\alpha,e_1 \rangle e)) \,\mathrm{v}\, ... \,\mathrm{v}\, (\mu = \langle i,\alpha,e_1,...,e_k \rangle \cdot (\mathrm{E}e)(e \,\epsilon\, \mathrm{Val} \cdot 0 \leq i \leq 1 \cdot \langle e,\mathrm{Prhd}^i,\alpha,e_1,...,e_k \rangle e)))$.

The "suitable" self-seekings are thus grounded in the aesthetic order, and improper ones are not. The proper conduct of life is thus, in a most definite sense, a matter of aesthetic harmony, each act, state, process, and so on, having its proper place in the valuations of the primordial nature.

4

Some writers view Whitehead's aesthetic order as involving only the EO's in abstraction from the AO's to which they apply. The aesthetic order is therewith handled somewhat in the manner of the "hierarchy" of EO's in the "Abstraction" chapter in *Science and the Modern World*. Surely there is an aesthetic order amongst just the EO's, of course, but it is derivative from the richer and more complex order that arises from the set just considered. In fact the order among the EO's *must* be regarded as derivative to be in harmony with the ontological principle (CE(xviii), *Process and Reality*, pp. 36-37), that all "reasons" are to be given in terms ultimately of AO's. In any case, Whitehead is quite explicit that the primordial vision must embrace all AO's. For example, he refers (*Process and Reality*, p. 373) to the "inevitable ordering of things, conceptually realized [valuated] in the nature of God." These "things" are surely no other than AO's. Also (p. 522) the "conceptual feelings which compose ... [the] primordial nature, exemplify in their subjective forms their mutual sensitivity and their subjective unity of subjective aim. These subjective forms

[3] A. N. Whitehead, *Religion in the Making* (The Macmillan Co., New York : 1926), p. 105.

are valuations determining the relative relevance [degree] of eternal objects for each occasion of actuality." Here occasions of actuality are merely AO's. And still more explicitly (p. 134), the *png* is "the concrescence of an unity of conceptual feelings, including among their data all eternal objects. The concrescence is directed by the subjective aim, that the subjective forms of the feeling shall be such as to constitute the eternal objects into relevant lures of feeling severally appropriate for all realizable basic conditions." Note that EO's are "included" among the data of the primordial valuations but also are "lures of feeling severally appropriate" for the AO's to which they apply.

When talking of God, and then only, Whitehead distinguishes between an AO and an actual entity (hereafter AE).[4] The AE's consist of all AO's plus God. God is thus an AE but not an AO. The reason is given by the somewhat special character of the *png*. The *png* (p. 134) "has no past," nor any present or future, for that matter, whereas all AO's do. "God differs from the other actual entities in the fact that Hume's principle, of the derivate character of conceptual feelings, does not hold for him." These feelings are thus truly "primordial."

Whitehead says, in one of his less felicitous paragraphs, that for God (pp. 134-135) [5] "the same threefold character" obtains as for any AO. But of course it is not the same at all.[6] We must consider separately the *png* and the *cng*. The *png* does not originate from the past actual world, it does not undergo concrescence in the same way that other AE's do, nor does it have a superjective character in the same sense. Distinctions of time are irrelevant for the *png* in virtue of its being primordial. On the other hand, its valuations are "with" all creation in the sense of constituting the initial subjective aim. The *png* is a concrescence only in the sense of being a fusion of conceptual prehensions, not in the sense of having "phases" such as originative (in past physical experience), creative, satisfactional, superjective, and so on. There is no "creativity" in the *png* as with AO's, except in the sense that all its primordial valuations are lures for creativity on the part of other AE's. Nor is the *png*'s "satisfaction" like that of other AE's, nor indeed is its "superjective character." One

---

[4] *Process and Reality*, p. 135.

[5] These two key pages were not commented on in III above.

[6] As observed by Professor W. H. Sheldon in his penetrating critical remarks in his seminars on Whitehead.

can use these words in connection with the *png* only metaphorically, it would seem.

"The consequent nature of God is the physical prehension by God of the actualities of the evolving universe." Here the distinction between the *cng* and the *cng^e* is relevant. The *cng^e* is the body of God up to and including *e*. The negative of *cng^e* is then merely -*cng^e*, so that

$$(e)((\sim e = cng \cdot \sim e = png) \supset cng = (cng^e \cup -cng^e)).$$

Only a *cng^e* may be said to "prehend" literally. For the *cng* as a whole to prehend some *e* is merely for *e* to be a part of it, which of course every non-primordial *e* is. Each -*cng^e* undergoes genuine concrescence in the same sense that any AO does. But *cng^e* does not. There is no physical past for it literally to prehend, it has no "actual world," and so on. And similarly for the *cng* as a whole. It "prehends" only in the sense of encompassing into its own internal constitution all AO's, prehensions, and so on, other than the primordial valuations.

"The 'superjective' nature of God is the character of the pragmatic value of his specific satisfaction qualifying the transcendent creativity in the various temporal instances." Here again we should distinguish the *png*, the *cng*, and each *cng^e*. The superjective nature of the *png* is its presence as an ideal influencing all becoming. The *cng* literally has no superjective nature but some of its proper parts do. In particular then each *cng^e* has its own "satisfaction" qualifying all *e'*'s in the subsequent world.

5

Let us return again to the notion of evil. "The kingdom of heaven is not the isolation of good from evil. It is the overcoming of evil by good. This transmutation of evil into good enters into the actual world by reason of the inclusion of the nature of God, which includes the ideal vision of each actual evil in the restoration of goodness. God has in his nature the knowledge of evil, of pain, and of degradation, but it is there as overcome with what is good. Every fact is what it is, a fact of pleasure, of joy, of pain, or of suffering. In its union with God that fact is not a total loss, but on its finer side is an element to be woven immortally into the rhythm of mortal things. Its very evil becomes a stepping stone in the all-embracing ideals of God." [7]

---

[7] *Religion in the Making*, p. 155.

In *Process and Reality* (p. 525), a similar point is made. "The revolts of destructive evil, purely self-regarding, are dismissed into their triviality of merely individual facts; and yet the good they did achieve in individual joy, in individual sorrow, in the introduction of needed contrast, is yet saved by its relation of the completed whole. The image — and it is but an image — the image under which this operative growth of God's nature is best conceived, is that of a tender care that nothing be lost."

How are we to understand these two famous passages and this doctrine that the function of evil is that it be "overcome" by good?

The "data" of the primordial prehensions are the EO's in their "relative relevance" to the AO's to which they apply. Most of these AO's undergo evil in the sense that the primordial valuations concerning them are not realized. An AO is thus partly evil, but perhaps also partly good. Each AO is the fusion of its prehensions; the "feeler" is "emergent" from the totality of its own feelings. Those of its prehensions that accord with the primordial ones concerning it are good or perfect, otherwise evil. Each AO is thus partially perfect, as it should be, if some of its prehensions are good. If good prehensions predominate to some considerable extent, the AO is presumably as good as it can be, as good as circumstances permit. But evil is rampant everywhere, so that in actuality evil prehensions gain the ascendancy. Thus by and large most AO's come out as evil, as "what in the temporal world is mere wreckage."

The interesting fact is that even evil AO's are among the "data" for further primordial valuations. There is no exclusiveness in the *png* in this regard. The valuations are not merely of the good but of the evil as well. Each evil AO is "covered by God," transmuted into good, by being given its proper role, so to speak, in the primordial ordering. Of course the good that overcomes evil may itself be overcome by evil, only to be overcome again by good primordially. Whitehead's seemingly metaphorical way of writing about evil is thus seen to have a very precise theoretical foundation.

6

The foregoing cosmological grounding for perfection and evil is by no means simple and encompasses a vast theory of extraordinary scope. The doctrine of God is supposed to be the "chief exemplification" of metaphysical principles and not an exception "invoked to save their collapse." Even so, the uneasy feeling arises that the primordial valuations in particular instances are arbitrary. They might be this way but they might also be that. There seems no compulsion for them to be just what they are and not otherwise.

In *Science and the Modern World* (p. 256) Whitehead comments that "there cannot be value without antecedent standards of value, to discriminate the acceptance or rejection of what is before the envisaging mode of activity [the AO]. Thus there is an antecedent limitation among values, introducing contraries, grades, and oppositions. ... God is the ultimate limitation, and His existence is the ultimate irrationality. For no reason can be given for just that limitation which it stands in His nature to impose. God is not concrete, but He is the ground for concrete actuality. No reason can be given for the nature of God, because that nature is the ground of rationality."

This much discussed passage contains of course Whitehead's answer to the qualms expressed above. The God here is clearly the *png* who fixes "antecedent standards" of value. Qualms remain, however, for those who wish to maintain that the ultimate source of value should not itself be irrationally or arbitrarily grounded. One of the deepest and perennial traditions of human thought is to the effect that we do in fact wish to pursue our reason to an *O Altitudo*.

If the primordial valuations have only a fortuitous ground, why should they be accepted? Why should we even try to realize them in practice or to make behavior accord with them? To be sure, they provide moral order, but other sets of valuations would do that also. Just as there are variant moral orders, there of course are variant aesthetic orders also. There is no rational ground for one any more than for any other. Again, it is difficult to accept the view that the one dominant aesthetic order is merely grounded by primordial fiat.

Another line of criticism of the Whiteheadian doctrine is to the effect that the *png* consists merely of valuations. Whitehead never states just what form these valuations take. Above it was suggested that they may be expressed by means of 'should'. It is not altogether clear that they need be expressed in this way, however. 'Should' carries some kind of compulsion with it. The primordial valuations, however, are primarily "lures to feeling;" they lure but do not compel, or even for that matter persuade. Our highest ideals, however, are something more : they compel and carry their authenticity on their sleeves. An act of high moral rightness owes its integrity to more than the whim of a primordial fiat. The experience of a great work of art may be so compelling as to suggest total consonance with the entire cosmos. The values fit the cosmos most integrally and rationally, and not just fortuitously — so it might be urged.

The moral and aesthetic orders can be compelling in certain respects without God's being conceived as a despotic monarch. Just as "great art likes chains," in the phrase of Nadia Boulanger, so is moral behaviour unthinkable without coercive restraints. Augustine's 'Love God and do as you will' admonishes us to follow the primordial valuations and, whatever else we do, to do this above all. This admonition presupposes that there is some coercive benignity in the nature of things, as well as some cosmic beauty, that is on our side. But neither the *cng* nor the *png*, nor their logical sum, are therewith given attributes that "belong exclusively to Caesar."

Another difficulty is that Whitehead nowhere tells us how we are to know when we have hold of a primordial valuation. Let a valuation be verbally expressed. How can we tell whether it is primordial or not? Some criterion is needed here, or at least the suggestion of one. Valuations influence the stream of occasions by being prehended with such and such a subjective form, of course. But how primordial valuations differ from other types we are not told. By revelation? By special insight or intuition? By, in Tagore's phase, "the music they give"?

Witehead is nowhere very clear as to just what 'valuation' in connection with the primordial nature is supposed to cover. This is a pity, for the primordial nature and its role in the cosmos is left somewhat obscure as a result. Actually there would seem to be at least three important kinds of valuations to distinguish, which might be dubbed for the moment *demands*, *permissions*, and *desires*. A primordial valuation is a demand if what is valuated cannot fail to obtain. More particularly, where

$$\langle e, \text{Prhd}^1, \alpha, e_1, \ldots, e_n \rangle e,$$

e being a primordial demand, it must then obtain that $\alpha e_1, \ldots, e_n$. But if *e* is merely a primordial permission, this may or may not obtain. The contrast is essentially that of St. Augustine, that "nothing ... happens but by the will of the Omnipotent, He either permitting it to be done, or Himself doing it" (*Enchiridion ad Laurentium*, xcv). Moreover, primordial desires should be admitted, to accommodate the *summum bonum*, the *via crucis*, the *spes unica*, for each occasion with respect to the appropriate eternal objects. If *e* is a primordial desire, it is surely then a permission but not a demand. Likewise, any demand is a permission, but not of course conversely. It is only primordial desires that function as lures for feeling, as items in the divine persuasiveness. It is unfortunate that Whitehead does not give us an analysis of the primordial valuations and of the most important species of them. (Any numerical degrees < 1 have been disregarded here.)

7

For Whitehead 'perfect' functions adjectivally, as we have seen. There are perfect valuations and therewith perfect occasions. Further, the doctrine is a pluralism. There are many perfect entities. There is no one perfect entity, unless it be the *png* itself. But we are nowhere told that the *png* is "greater than" or "more perfect" than all else. On the contrary, the *png* is the repository of all perfection, but not strictly a perfect thing itself.

It is interesting to contrast this kind of a view concerning perfection with that of Fitch, which harks back in essentials to that of St. Anselm. God, for St. Anselm, it will be recalled is "id, quo maius cogitari non potest." This notion is couched in terms of a relation of *being greater than*, and the celebrated ontological argument presupposes suitable principles concerning that relation.[8] Fitch speaks of the relation of *being more nearly perfect than*, but this is essentially the same. Fitch goes even further and speaks of *degrees of perfection* but makes no essential use of this. He seeks to establish rather the principle, if such it be, that "if it is possible that something is perfect, then the attribute perfection is itself perfect." He uses for this purpose not only a modal logic but a doctrine of "attributes" of such a kind that some are allowed to apply to themselves.

Note that the Whiteheadian doctrine, in contrast, can be couched in terms of the standard logic, as is shown by the foregoing. No modal logic is needed and no deviant logic of any kind. The advantages of hewing to the standard logic are great and have eloquently been spelled out recently by Quine.[9]

A methodological critique of the deviant kind of approach has been

[8] See VIII below.

[9] See W. V. Quine, *Philosophy of Logic* (Prentice-Hall, Englewood Cliffs, N.J. : 1970) and "On Quine's *Philosophy of Logic*," in *Events, Reference, and Logical Form.*

well provided by Whitehead himself. "You cannot rise above the adequacy of the terms you employ. A dogma may be true in the sense that it expresses such interrelations of the subject matter as are expressible within the set of ideas employed. ... Progress in truth — truth of science and truth of religion — is mainly a progress in the framing of concepts, in discarding artificial abstractions or partial metaphors, and in evolving notions which strike more deeply into the root of reality." [10]

Whitehead's comments here are based on extraordinary methodological insight. One can employ a given set of terms — variables, predicates, connectives, or deviant notions and the like, of whatever kind one wishes — but one can never rise above the "adequacy" of them. Do what one will with them, one should always seek terms that "strike more deeply into the root of reality" without "artificial abstraction." Now modal-model notions and methods, and set-theoretic ones, and intensional notions *sui generis*, are veritable paragons of artificiality and of abstraction, as is universally recognized even by their proponents, useful perhaps up to a certain point, but ultimately to be discarded in favor of more adequate ones.[11] Half-way abstractions are useful in science; in fact science is impossible without them. They can have no place in philosophy, however. Methodological wisdom requires that we recognize this difference and not demand of the one what belongs more properly to the other.

Philosophy may be regarded as the endeavor to characterize in an all-embracing system, in the clearest possible terms and on the basis of the clearest possible logic and without artificial abstraction, every item of human experience, from the loftiest to the lowly, as well as to provide suitable methodological foundations for the humanistic disciplines and for the sciences in their totality. The most adequate terms for this formidable task are those that arise immediately out of the subject-matter at hand, suitable non-logical predicates, namely (many of them pragmatic in nature) that readily lend themselves to being formalized or characterized on the basis of standard logic.

It might be thought that in the deviant approach some of the difficulties urged above against Whitehead could be overcome. The doctrine of the perfection of perfection does not entail, in any clear

---

[10] *Religion in the Making*, p. 131.

[11] For a multiplicity of arguments against deviancy, see *Belief, Existence, and Meaning*, especially Chapter III.

way, however, a doctrine of value where values are either compelling or as the objects of lure. As a result, no connection with the realm of moral or aesthetic order is forthcoming, without anyhow a good deal of further elaboration.

8

Let us reflect a little more fully now upon a few items concerned with Fitch's general conception of what philosophy is and the relation of logic to it.

Fitch believes that "symbolic logic will eventually make possible new advances in value theory, epistemology, and philosophy which will be comparable with the advances that traditional mathematics, especially after the advent of calculus, has made possible in the natural sciences," and that the "study of logical systems is leading more and more philosophers to view the world in terms of relations, attributes, classes and propositions, and to study the structure of the world in terms of these categories ..." [12] It is interesting to note that this view is very close to that of Whitehead in his lecture "Mathematics and the Good." [13] Mathematics is there spoken of in the very broad sense of "the intellectual analysis of types of pattern" and the context makes clear that this is in essentials modern logic. "Mathematics" in this sense "is the most powerful technique for the understanding of pattern, and for the analysis of the relationships of patterns. ... If civilization continues to advance, in the next two thousand years the overwhelming novelty in human thought will be the dominance of mathematical understanding." By 'pattern' here is not meant a Platonic archetype or paradigm but rather a complex structure of relations among entities as characterized within a suitable logical system, with its non-logical relations, classes, and so on.

Fitch's "sketch" is essentially Whiteheadian, but with what he calls 'primary occasions' taking the place of Whitehead's AO's. Also Fitch's view admits "substances" that are not further reducible.[14] Primary occasions, unlike the AO's, are likewise indivisible and ato-

---

[12] F. B. Fitch, "Sketch of a Philosophy," in *The Relevance of Whitehead*, ed. by I. Leclerc (George Allen and Unwin, London : 1961).

[13] In *The Philosophy of Alfred North Whitehead*, ed. by P. A. Schilpp.

[14] Cf. the methods suggested in *Logic, Language, and Metaphysics*, Chapters VII and VIII.

mic. AO's are potentially divisible into spatio-temporal parts, ultimately into space-time points. The primary occasions, however, are
not so divisible, and in effect are made to play the role of space-time
points themselves.

Let 'p', 'p_1', 'p_2', and so on, be variables for primary occasions
ad 's', 's_1', 's_2', and so on, for "substances." Fitch uses non-logical
primitives as follows. "There is a relation of immediate causation
[IC] holding among primary occasions and ordering them into a
space-time somewhat like that envisaged in Einstein's General Theory
of Relativity ..." The primary occasions are themselves spatio-
temporal units and space-time itself is simply their "relatedness"
characterized presumably in terms of a suitable pattern. "Another
important relation among primary occasions in the relation [ISP] of
immediate substantival predecessor." This could also be referred to
as the relation of immediate *genidentical* predecessor for it "holds
from any primary occasion to the next primary occasion that is an
occasion of the same substance." Clearly, where 'p Of s' expresses
that p is a primary occasion *of* the substance s, we should have that
$$(p_1)(p_2)(p_1 \text{ ISP } p_2 \supset (Es)(p_1 \text{ Of } s \cdot p_2 \text{ Of } s)).$$

"A whole chain of primary occasions related serially by the relation
of immediate causation constitutes a causal chain of occasions."
In order that the "chain" be of the same logical type as the occasions
themselves, the chain may be regarded merely as the logical sum,
or fusion, of the primary occasions in the series. Let now an *occasion*
be any sum of primary occasions, and let 'o', 'o_1', and so on, be variables for such, in particular, then, for primary occasions and occasions.
Thus, to explicate Fitch's notion, we may perhaps let

'$\text{CsChn}_{IC} \, o$' abbreviate '$((p_1)(p_2)((p_1 \text{ P } o \cdot p_2 \text{ P } o) \supset (p_1 = p_2$
v p_1 *IC p_2 v p_2 *IC p_1)) $\cdot$ (Ep)$o = \text{Fu}'\hat{p}_1(p_1$ *IC p v p *IC p_1))'.
An occasion o is thus a causal chain, according to this definition, if
any two distinct primary occasions p_1 and p_2 that are parts of it are
such that p_1 bears the ancestral *IC of IC to p_2 or conversely, and there
is a p such that o itself is the fusion of all primary occasions that p
bears *IC to or conversely. (On the ancestral of a relation, see *Principia
Mathematica*, *90.)

Fitch is not explicit as to what a "chain" is nor as to just how we are
to construe 'related serially by the relation of immediate causation'.
The relation IC is of course not a serial relation. Although it is
clearly transitive and asymmetric it is not connected. The first clause
in the definiens of the definition just given requires in effect that IC is

connected among the primary occasions that are parts of o. This
definition thus seems to capture what Fitch perhaps intends.

"A whole chain of occasions joined together serially by this relation
[ISP] constitutes a substance enduring through time." Some causal
chains are determined by IC, others by ISP. Thus we now let

$$\text{'Chn}_{ISP}\ o\text{'}$$

be defined as above but with 'ISP' replacing 'IC' in the definiens.
Then presumably it holds that

$$(s)s = \text{Fu'}\hat{o}(\text{Chn}_{ISP}\ o\ \cdot\ (p)(p\ \text{P}\ o \supset p\ \text{Of}\ s)).$$

If we are to construe 'constitute' here as 'is identical with' the
statement of what Fitch intends would seem to be that any substance
s is the sum of all ISP-chains whose primary-occasion parts bear
Of to s.

Fitch contends that "every such substantival chain, or substance,
is also a causal chain, but not every causal chain is a substance."
But clearly not every o such that $\text{Chn}_{ISP}\ o$ is a substance. Nor is every
o such that $\text{Chn}_{ISP}\ o$ also such that $\text{CsChn}_{IC}\ o$. Surely substances
can contain temporally adjacent primary occasions without there
being causal connection between them. Some primary occasion
contained in my right foot may bear ISP to some occasion contained
in my left hand, but it does not bear IC to it. Construct a temporal
chain now of primary occasions containing first an occasion of my
right foot, then one of my left hand, then one of my right foot,
and so on. Such a chain o is a Chn_{ISP} but not a CsChn_{IC}. Fitch seems
to neglect here the possibility that substances may contain contempo-
rary primary occasions as parts.

Among the "substances" certain ones are called 'selves' or 'souls'
so that right off a kind of mind-body dualism sets in. However, we
need not worry about the proliferation of different types of entities
here, for all of them are ultimately, according to Fitch elsewhere,
reducible to propositions.[15] A suitable defined predicate, say 'S', is
needed so that 'S s' expresses that s is a soul.

For Fitch there is at most a denumerable number of primary
occasions. This accords with his constructivistic approach to real
number theory. Space-time and measurement are thus handled accordingly. Consider a causal chain, say a light-ray path, such that no
two causally successive primary occasions of it are in any other causal
chain. Or one could consider a substantival chain no two primary

[15] F. B. Fitch, "Propositions as the Only Realities,"

occasions of which are contemporary, call it a '*linear* substantival chain'. For such chains, "there exists a unique number associated with any two primary occasions on that chain, namely the number n of primary occasions lying between them on that chain." If the chain is a linear substantival one, "consider two occasions in the life history of ... [that] substance and consider the number n of primary occasions lying between them serially in that life-history. This number n can be viewed as a measure of the absolute amount of time elapsed between those two occasions in the life-history of that substance, as from the standpoint of that substance itself. This is the basis for saying that time has magnitude and in measurable." In fact for Fitch this is the basis of saying that there is any such thing as time at all. And similarly *mutatis mutandis* for space or space-time. Space-time emerges from the "relatedness" of primary occasions and substances and hence methods must be developed of constructing or defining co-ordinate systems rather than the other way around, of explaining "this relatedness in terms of antecedently given co-ordinate systems."

The number n here must presumably be an *integer*, not a fraction or an irrational, the primary occasions not being subdivisible. If so, all temporal intervals are integral, and spatial ones also. Thus if 10 is the number assigned to the occasions lying between (and including) the occasions p_1 and p_2 and also the number assigned to the occasion lying between (and including) p_1 and p_3 taken at right angles so to speak (whatever this means), then of course there is no integer n to be assigned to the occasions lying between (and including) p_2 and p_3. The point is of course that $\sqrt{200}$ is not an integer. Fitch is well aware of this kind of difficulty and thinks nonetheless that the full real-number system is not needed for the theory of measurement. The point is moot and a good deal of work needs yet to be done to show how modern science with its highly sophisticated methods of measurement can forego the real numbers *in toto*. We shall return to this topic in a moment.

Fitch's "sketch" is fascinating and merits more discussion and elaboration than can be given here. It should be noted, however, that although deviant logic is actually made use of, the main contentions of the sketch in no way depend upon it. The doctrine of primary occasions, substances, of immediate causality, and so on, can be formulated within the confines of orthodox logic. As the system is developed, however, into the theory of perception and of knowledge, Fitch's deviant approach becomes essential — or at least, so it might be thought. But alternative mays of approaching these intentional subjects are at hand without resort to deviancy, as is now well known.

9

In the preceding paper, it will be recalled, a method of handling geometric entities as idealized or fictional constructs was suggested. The method has its roots in Whitehead's notion of a coordinate division. It is based essentially on a process of *extrapolation* whereby one builds up points in terms ultimately of *point events*. Now point events are very much like Whitehead's actual occasions and Fitch's primary ones. What is called 'protogeometry' consists of notions and principles by means of which this extrapolation is made explicit. It is interesting to observe that with extrapolation we can build up the non-denumerable on a denumerable basis, but without of course using sets, classes, relations, or the like, as values for variables.

In terms of protogeometry, let us sketch now what might be called 'protoanalysis' or 'proto-real-number theory'. In this way, a method of providing for the real numbers as hypothetical constructs will be given — for the whole theory, not just for the fragment of it used by Fitch.

Let '$Pt_g\ e$' and '$L_g\ e$' express that the geometer g takes the "entity" e as a point or as a line respectively, as in the previous paper. The e here is always *de facto* the null entity, but person g regards it or takes it to be the required kind of geometrical entity. In other words, he takes e under a suitable hypothetical attitude.

In protogeometry the theory of a one-dimensional continuum of points on a line can be developed before branching off into the complexities required for a full axiomatization of some special geometry, Euclidean, Riemannian, or whatever. The leading idea now is simply to allow the geometer or person g to regard a point as corresponding with a real number, different ones with different ones, in such a way that all talk of real numbers becomes merely a certain way of talking about points. To see this, let us consider at once the primitives required.

First, we allow g to pick out some one line as the real-number axis. Thus

'$Ax_g\ e$'

may express that g takes e as the axis. Clearly then

$(e)(\text{Ax}_g\ e \supset \text{L}_g\ e)$

and

$(\text{E}e)(\text{Ax}_g\ e \cdot (e')\ (\text{Ax}_g\ e' \supset e =_g e'))$.

Thus there is one and only one entity that g takes as axis and that is taken by him to be a line. Also

$$\text{'Zero}_g\ e\text{'}$$

and

$$\text{'One}_g\ e\text{'}$$

express that g takes e to be the real numbers 0 and 1 respectively. Here also

$(e)(\text{Zero}_g\ e \supset (\text{Pt}_g\ e \cdot e\ \text{On}_g\ (\iota e' \cdot \text{Ax}_g\ e')))$

and

$(\text{E}e)(\text{Zero}_g\ e \cdot (e')(\text{Zero}_g\ e' \supset e =_g e'))$.

(Here '$e =_g e'$' expresses that g takes the hypothetical entities e and e' as the same, and '$e\ \text{On}_g\ e'$' expresses that g takes the "point" e to lie on the "line" e'.) And similarly for 1. Also of course

$(e)(e')((\text{Zero}_g\ e \cdot \text{One}_g\ e') \supset \sim e =_g e')$.

Next let

$$\text{'}e_1 <_g e_2\text{'}$$

express that g takes the "real number" e_1 to be less than the "real number" e_2, and

$$\text{'}e_1\ \text{Bet}_g\ e_2,e_3\text{'},$$

that g takes e_1 to be "between" e_2 and e_3. Clearly then

$(e_1)(e_2)(e_1 <_g e_2 \supset (e_1\ \text{On}_g\ (\iota e \cdot \text{Ax}_g\ e) \cdot e_2\ \text{On}_g\ (\iota e \cdot \text{Ax}_g\ e) \cdot \sim e_1 =_g e_2 \cdot (\text{E}e_3)e_3\ \text{Bet}_g\ e_1,e_2))$.

In terms or '$<_g$' of course suitable ordering principles can be given. This will be done in a moment. The principles given thus far are merely *entitival*, stating the kinds of entities being dealt with.

Let now

$$\text{'}(e_1 + e_2)_g\ e\text{'}$$

and

$$\text{'}(e_1 \times e_2)_g\ e\text{'}$$

expresses primitively that person g takes e to be the sum or product, respectively, of the "real numbers" e_1 and e_2. Then of course

$(e_1)(e_2)(e)((e_1 + e_2)_g\ e \supset (e_1\ \text{On}_g\ (\iota e \cdot \text{Ax}_g\ e) \cdot e_2\ \text{On}\ (\iota e \cdot \text{Ax}_g\ e) \cdot e\ \text{On}_g\ (\iota e \cdot \text{Ax}_g\ e)))$,

and similarly for '$\times$'.

10

It is known that with '1','0','<','+' and '×' as primitives, the real number system may be axiomatized on the basis of standard first-order logic.[16] In particular then, Tarski's axioms may be adapted here as follows. Let

'$NR_g\ e$' abbreviate '$e\ On_g\ (\iota e'\ \cdot\ Ax_g\ e')$'

so that the definiendum here expresses in effect that g takes e to be a real number.

First we have axioms of ordering.

*Ax*1. $(e_1)(e_2)(NR_g\ e_1\ \cdot\ NR_g\ e_2\ \cdot\ \sim\ e_1 =_g e_2) \supset (e_1 <_g e_2 \vee e_2 <_g e_1))$.

*Ax*2. $(e_1)(e_2)(e_1 <_g e_2 \supset \sim e_2 <_g e_1)$.

*Ax*3. $(e_1)(e_2)(e_3)((e_1 <_g e_2\ \cdot\ e_{2g} <_g e_3) \supset e_1 <_g e_3)$.

Next we have axioms concerning addition.

*Ax*4. $(e_1)(e_2)((NR_g\ e_1\ \cdot\ NR_g\ e_2) \supset (Ee)(NR_g\ e\ \cdot\ (e_1 + e_2)_g\ e\ \cdot\ (e')((e_1 + e_2)_g\ e' \supset e' =_g e)))$.

*Ax*5. $(e)(e_1)(e_2)(((e_1 + e_2)_g\ e\ \cdot\ Zero_g\ e_2) \supset e =_g e_1)$.

*Ax*6. $(e)(e')(e_1)(e_2)(((e_1 + e_2)_g\ e\ \cdot\ (e_2 + e_1)_g\ e') \supset e =_g e')$.

*Ax*7. $(e)(e')(e'')(e''')(e_1)(e_2)(e_3)(((e_2 + e_3)_g\ e\ \cdot\ (e_1 + e)_g\ e'\ \cdot\ (e_1 + e_2)_g\ e''\ \cdot\ (e'' + e_3)_g\ e''') \supset e' =_g e''')$.

*Ax*4 is the principle of the unique existence of the sum of two reals. *Ax*5 states in effect that any real number added to 0 is merely that real number. *Ax*6 and *Ax*7 are respectively commutative and associative laws for real-number addition. Next we have the principle of monotony for addition.

*Ax*8. $(e_1)(e_2)(e)(e')((e_1 <_g e_2\ \cdot\ (e_3 + e_1)_g\ e\ \cdot\ (e_3 + e_2)_g\ e') \supset e <_g e')$.

Next we have principles concerning multiplication.

*Ax*9. $(e_1)(e_2)((NR_g\ e_1\ \cdot\ NR_g\ e_2) \supset (Ee)(NR_g\ e\ \cdot\ (e_1 \times e_2)_g\ e\ \cdot\ (e')((e_1 \times e_2)_g\ e' \supset e' =_g e)))$.

*Ax*10. $(e_1)(e_2)(e)(((e_1 \times e_2)_g\ e\ \cdot\ One_g\ e_2) \supset e =_g e_1)$.

*Ax*11. $(e_1)(e_2)(e)(e')(((e_1\ (e_2)_g\ e\ \cdot\ (e_2 \times e_1)_g\ e') \supset e =_g e')$.

*Ax*12. $(e_1)(e_2)(e_3)(e)(e')(e'')(e''')(((e_2 \times e_3)_g\ e\ \cdot\ (e_1 \times e)_g\ e'\ \cdot\ (e_1 \times e_2)_g\ e''\ \cdot\ (e'' \times e_3)_g\ e''') \supset e' =_g e''')$.

*Ax*13. $(e)(e')(e_1)(e_2)(e_3)(e_4)((Zero_g\ e_1\ \cdot\ e_1 <_g e_2\ \cdot\ e_3 <_g e_4\ \cdot\ (e_2 \times e_3)_g\ e\ \cdot\ (e_2 \times e_4)_g\ e') \supset e <_g e')$.

---

[16] Cf. A. Tarski, *Introduction to Logic* (Oxford University Press, New York: 1941), Chapter X.

$Ax9$ is the principle of the unique existence of the product of two reals. $Ax10$ is the principle of multiplication by 1, and $Ax11$ and $Ax12$ are respectively commutative and associative laws. $Ax12$ is the principle of monotony for multiplication. Also we have the distributive law as follows.

$Ax14$. $(e_1)(e_2)(e_3)(e)(e')(e'')(e''')(e'''')(((e_2 + e_3)_g \ e \ \cdot (e_1 \times e)_g \ e' \ \cdot (e_1 \times e_2)_g \ e'' \ \cdot (e_1 \times e_3)_g \ e''' \cdot (e'' + e''')_g \ e'''') \supset e' =_g e'''')$.

The following two principles postulate respectively the existence of the difference and the quotient of real numbers.

$Ax15$. $(e_1)(e_2)(Ee_2)(Ee)((e_2 + e_3)_g \ e \ \cdot e_1 =_g e)$.

$Ax16$. $(e_1)(e_2)(\sim \text{Zero}_g \ e_2 \supset (Ee_3)(Ee)((e_2 \times e_3)_g \ e \ \cdot e_1 =_g e))$.

Finally, we have the Dedekindian principle as follows.

$Ax17$. $(\sim F = \Lambda \ \cdot \sim G = \Lambda \ \cdot (e)(F e \supset \text{NR}_g \ e) \ \cdot (e)(G e \supset \text{NR}_g \ e) \ \cdot (e_1)(e_2)((F \ e_1 \ \cdot G \ e_2) \supset e_1 <_g e_2)) \supset (Ee_3)(e_1)(e_2)((F \ e_1 \ \cdot G \ e_2 \ \cdot \sim e_3 =_g e_1 \ \cdot \sim e_3 =_g e_2) \supset (e_1 <_g e_3 \ \cdot e_3 <_g e_2))$.

It can easily be verified that $Ax1$-$Ax17$ plus the principles of proto-analysis given above, together with such principles of protogeometry as are needed, provide for the full theory of the first-order arithmetic of real numbers. The second-order arithmetic of real numbers admits also variables and quantifiers over sets and functions of real numbers, but these are not provided for here. This limitation is not so very serious, however, for the first-order theory presumably suffices for most of the needs of the physical sciences, in particular for the purpose of measurement.[17]

To summarize. The philosophy of real arithmetic that emerges from the foregoing has the following features. Real numbers are regarded as subjective or "mental" entities, not as real abstract objects in the objective world. The only ontology admitted is that of protogeometry, in particular, some one "line" picked out as the real-number axis. The primitives required are of a pragmatic kind, a paramenter for the "user" g occurring in all the atomic sentential forms. The entire theory is couched within event logic as extended with the new primitives. Unrestricted quantifiers over the reals are admitted. The method here contrasts sharply with other ways of handling the reals; the real numbers are not regarded as sets or classes of rationals (as in set-theoretic accounts) nor are they taken as values for a special kind of variable (as in Tarski's account). The theory here is "constructivistic"

---

[17] See the author's "In Defense of Nominalism", in *Events, Reference, and Logical Form*.

in a kind of Kantian sense, but not in the sense that the reals are constructed or built out of some prior kind of number (rational or integral). Strictly here there are no such things as real numbers — they are mere fictions or hypothetical constructs, in no way entities in their own right. Nonetheless, the uses to which real numbers are ordinarily put in science may be provided for here without difficulty. The view is thus a kind of pragmatic, instrumentalist fictionalism.

In this paper various topics concerned with mathematics and the good have been brought together within a common framework. There has been a sympathetic discussion of some aspects of Whitehead's theory of evil and perfection, with some occasional critical remarks. There has been a sympathetic discussion of some aspects of Fitch's "sketch" of a general philosophy with some occasional remarks. Finally, it has been shown how event logic itself may be extended to accommodate a full first-order theory of real numbers. Note incidentally that although sets have been used fundamentally in the discussion of Whitehead and Fitch, no use has been made of them in the discussion of real numbers.

VIII

ON THE LOGICAL STRUCTURE OF THE
ONTOLOGICAL ARGUMENT

"ERGO, DOMINE DEUS, QUI DAS FIDEI INTELLECTUM, DA MIHI UT,
QUANTUM SCIS EXPIDERE, INTELLIGAM QUIA ES, SICUT CREDIMUS, ET HOC
ES QUOD CREDIMUS."

1

The ontological argument of Saint Anselm, one of the most famous
in the entire history of philosophy, has fascinated men's minds for
centuries. And yet, as Hartshorne [1] makes abundantly clear, much
of its subtlety has been missed by some of the keenest commentators.
Although it has been discussed again and again, little work seems
to have been done, even up to the moment, in probing at all deeply
the logical forms needed for an exact statement. [2] Part of this is due
no doubt to the subtlety of the argument itself, but part of it is due
to the fact that the key ideas involved are not of the kind that easily
lend themselves to being handled within the standard kinds of logic.

Let us first explore *de novo* what seem to be the essentials of the
argument, within event logic, and then compare it with Anselm's
text, especially the *Proslogium*, Chapter II and III. In other words,
a kind of idealized ontological argument is first given in the light of
which the actual text may be examined. To say *precisely* what "the"
ontological argument is is by no means easy. Hence it seems better to
start with an idealized version.

In event logic, it will be recalled, a predicate for existence is available. Thus '$E!e$' expresses that e is not null. An intentional relation
of conceiving may be introduced so that

$$\text{'}e \text{ Cncv } e_1, e_2\text{'}$$

expresses that person e conceives e_1 under the linguistic description e_2.
(See X below.) The e_2 here is a predicate, so that the whole form

---

[1] Charles Hartshorne, *Anselm's Discovery* (Open Court, LaSalle, III, : 1965).
[2] Cf. Desmond Henry, *The Logic of Saint Anselm* (Clarendon Press, Oxford :
1967).

expresses that person e conceives e_2 to apply to the entity e_1. Also let

$$\text{`}e \text{ Able } e_1,e_2\text{'} \quad \text{or} \quad \text{`}e \text{ Cpbl } e_1,e_2\text{'}$$

express that person e is able (capable) or has the capacity or ability to do e_1 under the description e_2. Finally, let 'e_1 Gr e_2' express that e_1 is greater than e_2 in the Anselmic sense.

The key definition to be provided for is :

'Deus' abbreviates 'id, quo maius cogitari non potest'.

Such a definition is to be of an individual constant by means of a Russellian description. The existence and uniqueness of the entity described must be established before such a definition is useful.

Let us speak hereafter of the *Unsurpassable*, following Hartshorne. The Unsurpassable is that than which no greater can be conceived. Thus we may let

'Uns e' abbreviate '$\sim (Ee')(Ee_1)(Ee_2)(Ee_3)(e_2$ Des $e_1 \cdot e_3$ Des $e \cdot$ Per $e_1 \cdot e_1$ Able $e',^\ulcorner\langle e_2,\text{Cncv},e_3,\text{`}\{e_4\ni(Ee_5)e_5 \text{ Gr } e_4\}\text{'}\rangle\urcorner)$'.

The 'Des' here of course stands for the relation of designation, and 'Per e_1' expresses that e_1 is a human person. (Note here also the need for Quine's quasi-quotes.[3]) This definition in effect introduces as Unsurpassable any entity e such that no one is able to have a conceiving of anything under the description of its being greater than e.

Clearly as meaning postulates concerning 'Cncv' and 'Able' we have that

$$(e)(e_1)(e_2)(e \text{ Cncv } e_1,e_2 \supset \text{Per } e)$$

and

$$(e)(e_1)(e_2)(e \text{ Able } e_1,e_2 \supset \text{Per } e).$$

2

How now could it be established that there exists one and only one unsurpassable entity? — for it is this that the argument seeks to show. Let us find, if we can, reasonable premisses from which this conclusion would follow logically.

First, it seems reasonable to assume that at least one person conceives of something under the predicate 'Uns'. Thus the first premiss may be to the effect that

(1) $(Ee)(Ee')e \text{ Cncv } e',\text{`Uns'}$.

---

[3] On quasi-quotes or corners, see W. V. Quine, *Mathematical Logic* (W. W. Norton Co., New York : 1940), pp. 33 ff. or *Truth and Denotation*, pp. 34 f.

This is a very weak assumption : at least one person in the whole history of the cosmos has (or has had or will have) this conception.

Next it seems reasonable to assume that any entity that is unsurpassable exists in the sense of being non-null.

(2) $(e)(\text{Uns } e \supset E!e)$.

Further, there can be no two unsurpassable entities.

(3) $(e)(e')((\text{Uns } e \cdot \text{Uns } e') \supset e = e')$.

Finally, anything conceived as unsurpassable must itself be unsurpassable.

(4) $(e)(e')(e \text{ Cncv } e','\text{Uns'} \supset \text{Uns } e')$.

Clearly now, from (1) and (4) it follows that

$$(Ee')\text{Uns } e'.$$

and from this with (2) that

$$(Ee')(\text{Uns } e' \cdot E!e'),$$

and finally, from this and (3), that

$$E!(\iota e \cdot \text{Uns } e),$$

where 'E!' is essentially as in *Principia Mathematica*, *14.02. (1) here might be regarded as a statement of fact, and (2), (3), and (4) as meaning postulates concerning 'Uns'.

3

'Uns' here, however, is a defined predicate. The question arises therefore as to whether (2), (3), and (4) can be proved from prior postulates governing the notions occurring in the definiens of the definition. Consider first (2). The following is a reasonable assumption concerning the null entity.

(5) $(e)(\text{Per } e \supset e \text{ Cncv N,}`\{e_4 \ni (Ee_5)e_5 \text{ Gr } e_4\}')$

or equivalently

$(e)(e_1)((\text{Per } e \cdot \sim E!e_1) \supset e \text{ Cncv } e_1, `\{e_5 \ni (Ee_5)e_4 \text{ Gr } e_4\}')$.

Everyone conceives the null entity, or any non-existent entity, under the description of there being something greater than it. Also if a person e conceives such and such an action or event or entity then he is *able* to conceive it. A general principle concerning 'Able' is clearly then that

(6) $(e)(e_1)(e_2)(e')(e'')((e \text{ Cncv } e_1,e_2 \cdot e' \text{ Des } e \cdot e'' \text{ Des } e_1) \supset (Ee_3)e$ Able $e_3,\ulcorner\langle e',\text{Cncv},e'',e_2\rangle\urcorner)$.

If one actually conceives such and such then he is able to conceive such and such. Hence in particular, it may be proved that

(7) $\sim$ Uns N,

if we note that

(8) $(e)((\text{Per } e \text{ v } e = \text{N}) \supset (Ee')e' \text{ Des } e)$.

And hence also (2). Thus (2) is provable on the assumption (5) and the general principle (6) concerning 'Able', together with the designation principle (8).

How now about (4)? Not much has been said about the relational predicate 'Cncv'. Clearly, however, conceiving here might be construed veridically, in the sense that what is conceived is true. More particularly, (1) would then be supposed to state that someone e truly conceives something e' under the description 'Uns', not in just the sense that he really has this conception but furthermore that the predicate 'Uns' truly applies to e'. Let us speak of conception in this sense as *veridical*. Let

'e VCncv e_1,e_2' abbreviate '$(Ee')(Ee_3)(e' \text{ Des } e_1 \cdot e \text{ Cncv } e_1,e_2 \cdot e_3 \text{ C } e_2,e' \cdot \text{Tr } e_3)$',

where 'Tr' is the predicate for truth and 'C' for concatenation. The definiendum reads 'e veridically conceives e_2 to apply to e_1'. Then (1) could be strengthened as follows.

(1') $(Ee)(Ee')e \text{ VCncv } e',\text{'Uns'}$.

From (1'), it follows that

(4') $(e)(e')(e \text{ VCncv } e',\text{'Uns'} \supset \text{Uns } e')$,

using the Tarski paradigm for truth.

Finally, now, what about the uniqueness principle (3)? This seems to rest upon two assumptions, one concerning truth and conceivability, and the other concerning the relation Gr of being greater than. Let us consider the second first. Clearly

(9) $(e)(e')((\sim (Ee'')e'' \text{ Gr } e \cdot \sim (Ee'')e'' \text{ Gr } e') \supset e = e')$.

If e and e' are both such that there is no greater, then they are the same. In the scale of entities related by Gr, no two are the greatest. Also, it may be assumed that

(10) $(e_1)(e_2)(e_3)(e)((\text{PredConOne } e_2 \cdot e_1 \text{ Des } e \cdot \text{Tr } e_3 \cdot e_3 \text{ C } e_2,e_1)$
$\supset (Ee')(Ee'')(Ee_4)(e_4 \text{ Des } e' \cdot e' \text{ Able } e'',^{\ulcorner}\langle e_4,\text{Cncv},e_1,e_2\rangle^{\urcorner}))$,

where 'PredConOne e_2' expresses that e_2 is a one-place predicate constant. This states in effect that every truth is such that someone is able to conceive it. Truths are in principle conceivable — perhaps no one ever conceives all of them, but in principle they are all conceivable by someone or other.

On the basis of (9) and (10), (3) itself may be established as follows. First, note that

(11) $(e)((Ee'')e''$ Gr $e = \sim$ Uns $e),$
by (10). Then

$(e)(e')((\text{Uns } e \cdot \text{Uns } e') \supset (\sim (Ee'')e'' \text{ Gr } e \cdot \sim (Ee'')e'' \text{ Gr } e')),$
and hence (3) itself using (9).

The net result of the reflections thus far is that from (1') alone, together with the reasonable assumptions (5), (6), (9), (10), and standard principles of semantics, it may be established that

$$\text{E!}(\iota e \cdot \text{Uns } e).$$

4

The assumption (1'), however, seems too strong. It states not only that someone conceives something under the description 'Uns' but that he does so veridically. The point of the "Proof" — as Hartshorne calls it — however, is to derive the veridicality from the conceiving, so to speak. On the other hand, going back to (1), it seems that it is too weak, in requiring only that there be at least one person, rather than all, who have the given conception. Some premiss stronger than (1) but weaker than (1') seems needed as the most suitable.

Consider now the statement that
(1'') $(Ee')(e)(\text{Per } e \supset e \text{ Cncv } e',\text{'Uns'}),$
to the effect that there is some e' (possibly null) such that everyone, "even the fool," conceives it under the description 'Uns'. "Even the fool is convinced that something exists in the understanding, at least, than which nothing greater can be conceived." Note that (1'') in effect states only that there exists a conception of something unsurpassable, and not of course that there exists an unsurpassable thing. Conceptions are in effect merely entities under given descriptions and are handled here contextually. Hence the quantifier '(Ee)' here can be read 'there is a conception' and the whole of (1'') merely states that there is a conception if *id, quo maius cogitare non potest*. Let us explore now what can be derived from (1'').

Clearly if one is able to conceive of some entity under a predicate e_2 and it is true that whatever has e_2 also has a predicate e_3, then he is able to conceive of that entity under the description e_3. (He may not actually entertain this latter kind of a conception but he is *able* to do so.) Thus
(12) $(e)(e_1)(e_2)(e_3)(e_4)(e_5)((e_4 \text{ Des } e \cdot e_3 \text{ Des } e_1 \cdot \text{PredConOne } e_2 \cdot$
$\text{PredConOne } e_3 \cdot (Ee')e \text{ Able } e', \ulcorner \langle e_*, \text{Cncv}, e_5, e_2 \rangle \urcorner \cdot (Ee_6)(Ee_7)(Ee_8)(\text{Vbl}$

e_6 · e_7 C e_2,e_6 · e_8 C e_3,e_6 · Tr $\ulcorner(e_6)(e_7 \supset e_8)\urcorner)) \supset (Ee')e$ Able $e',\ulcorner\langle e_4,\text{Cncv},e_5,e_3\rangle\urcorner)$.

(Here 'Vbl e_6' merely expresses that the sign event e_4 is a variable.) Also clearly no one is able consistently to conceive an entity under some predicate as well as under its negation. He may of course imagine it, or picture it, or the like, under different descriptions, but he cannot conceive it so. Thus also

(13) $(e)(e_1)(e_2)(e_3)(e_4)(e_5))(e_4$ Des e · e_5 Des e_1 · PredConOne e_2 · e_3 Neg e_2 · $(Ee')e$ Able $e',\ulcorner\langle e_4,\text{Cncv},e_5,e_2\rangle\urcorner) \supset \sim (Ee')e$ Able e', $\ulcorner\langle e_4,\text{Cncv},e_5,e_3\rangle\urcorner)$.

Here 'e_3 Neg e_2' expresses that the one-place predicate e_3 is the negative of e_2. Thus, where e_2 is, say,

$$`\{e \ni \sim (Ee')e' \text{ Gr } e\}',$$

e_3 is

$$`\{e \ni (Ee')e' \text{ Gr } e\}'.$$

The principle (13) is a most reasonable assumption to the effect that we are not able to conceive entites under contradictory predicates. Were we able to do so our conceptions would lack the kind of stability that they are supposed to have.

5

If (6), (10), (12), (13), and (1'') *inter alia* be granted, the "Proof" may proceed as follows. First note that

$(e)(e_1)(e_4)(e_5)((e$ Cncv $e_1,$'Uns' · e_4 Des e · e_5 Des $e_1) \supset (Ee')e$ Able $e',\ulcorner\langle e_4,\text{Cncv},e_5,$'Uns'$\rangle\urcorner)$,

by (6). Recall now (11), or rather its concerve, that

$(e_1)($Uns $e_1 \supset \sim (Ee'')e''$ Gr $e_1)$,

which is provable from (10). Hence, using (12),

$(e)(e_1)(e_4)(e_5)((e$ Cncv $e_1,$'Uns' · e_4 Des e · e_5 Des $e_1) \supset (Ee')e$ Able $e',\ulcorner\langle e_4,\text{Cncv},e_5,`\{e_3 \ni \sim (Ee_2)e_2$ Gr $e_3\}'\rangle\urcorner)$.

But then, in view of (13), also

$(e)(e_1)(e_4)(e_5)((e$ Cncv $e_1,$'Uns' · e_4 Des e · e_5 Des $e_1) \supset \sim (Ee')e$ Able $e',\ulcorner\langle e_4,\text{Cncv},e_4,`\{e_3 \ni (Ee_2)e_2$ Gr $e_3\}'\rangle\urcorner)$.

Hence of course

$(e)(e_1)((e$ Cncv $e_1,$'Uns' · $(Ee_4)e_4$ Des e · $(Ee_5)e_5$ Des $e_1) \supset \sim (Ee')$ $(Ee_4)(Ee_5)(e_4$ Des e · e_5 Des e_1 · e Able $e',\ulcorner\langle e_4,\text{Cncv},e_5,`\{e_3 \ni (Ee_2)e_2$ Gr $e_3\}'\rangle\urcorner))$,

and thus, using again (8),

$(e_1)(e)(e$ Cncv $e_1,$'Uns' $\supset$ Uns $e_1).$

Thus we have the key principle (4), (2) and (3) being provable as above. Hence now we have that

E!$(\iota e \cdot$ Uns $e),$

on the assumption of $(1'')$. Of course, additional principles have been used, standard principles of logic and semantics, together with (5), (6), (9), (10), (12), and (13).

6

The validity of one rendering of the ontological argument has now been established. The question arises now of course concerning its soundness. Are the premisses true, or at least rationally acceptable in some sense? That they are could be argued as follows. (6) seems a quite fundamental principle concerning 'Cncv' and 'Able'. In fact it would be but a special case of a much more general principle concerning 'Able', namely, that

$(e)(e_1)((\text{Per } e \cdot F e \cdot e_1 \text{ Des } e) \supset (Ee')e \text{ Able } e', \ulcorner \langle e,F \rangle \urcorner),$

where in place of 'F' any one-place predicate applicable to persons is inserted. Whatever anybody actually does or is he is at least able to do or be. *Ab esse ad posse valet illatio.* (10) likewise seems acceptable as a reasonable principle concerning man's ability to conceive : every truth (of quasi-atomic form) is conceivable by someone, conceivable at least in principle even if never conceived in fact. It is a *Principle of Adequation*, to the effect that our minds are adequate to conceive truths, in the sense of having the ability to do so.

(12) and (13) are clearly acceptable principles concerning man's ability to conceive. If one is able to conceive an entity under one predicate and it is true that whatever has that one predicate has another, then he is surely able to conceive that entity under the other predicate. (12) is a *quasi-Modus Ponens Principle*, having a structure somewhat similar to that familiar rule of logic. (13) in turn is a kind of principle of consistency or stability requiring that our conceptions be such as not to admit conceivings under contradictory predicates (during the times under consideration). (13) need not rule out the possibility of conceptual change, of course, the latter being accommodated by suitable notational change.

We are left then with the need to justify only $(1'')$, (5), and (9). (5) would seem an acceptable principle concerning 'N' if the predicate 'Gr' is available in its medieval setting. Likewise no doubt for the uniqueness principle (9). In the intended sense for 'Gr', surely this principle is to be allowed. However, it if is rejected, the existence part of the "Proof" still holds. From (1'') it is provable that

$$(Ee)(\text{Uns } e \cdot E!e).$$

This provides a somewhat weakened form of argument, but still impressive enough perhaps to be called 'an ontological argument'.

The soundness of the proof thus seems to stand or fall with the acceptability of (1'') itself. Given 'Gr' in its Anselmic setting, (1'') no doubt helps to characterize it. There is a "concept" of the unsurpassable in the sense defined, not a concept of modern science or of common life, perhaps, but a concept nonetheless — at least this could well be contended and argued for. In any case, (1'') is clearly acceptable within the whole scheme of ideas within which Anselm was working.

7

Let us examine now key sentences in the *Proslogium*, especially II and III, in the light of the foregoing.[4]

"And, indeed," Anselm writes, "we believe that thou art a being than which nothing greater can be conceived," and the very fool who "hath said in his heart, there is no God" is to be included among the *we*. The net effect of the first paragraph of II, which is merely preliminary, is thus that

we Blv *Thou*,'Uns'.

Next, Anselm notes, "it is one thing for an object to be in the understanding, and another to understand that the object exists." Clearly

$$(e)(e_1)(e')(e'')((\langle e, \text{Cncv}, e_1, 'F' \rangle e' \cdot \langle e, \text{Cncv}, e_1, '\{e_2 \ni (F\ e_2 \cdot E!e_2)\}' \rangle e'') \supset \sim e' = e'').$$

Even "the fool is convinced that something exists in the understanding, at least, than which nothing greater can be conceived." Hence the presence of the universal quantifier in (1'') above, to range over everyone whatsoever, even "fools."

(1'') in fact seems to render the first statement of the crucial next paragraph explicit, the statement "... even the fool is convinced that something exists in the understanding ... than which nothing greater can be conceived." Further, "assuredly that than which nothing grea-

---

[4] The translations are from Saint Anselm, *Basic Writings* (Open Court, Chicago: 1962).

ter can be conceived, cannot exist in the understanding alone," Anselm notes. "For, suppose it exists in the understanding alone : then it can be conceived to exist in reality; which is greater." Thus we are to suppose that

(A) (e)(Uns $e \supset$ (Ee')((e_1)(e_2)(e_3)((e_2 Des e_1 $\cdot$ Per e_1 $\cdot$ e_3 Des e') $\supset$ (Ee'')e_1 Able e'',$\ulcorner\langle e_2$,Cncv,e_3,'$\{e_4\ni$(Uns e_4 $\cdot$ E!e_4)$\}$'$\rangle$'$\urcorner$) $\cdot$ e' Gr e)).

In the final paragraph Anselm draws the conclusion from (A) : "Therefore, if that, than which nothing greater can be conceived, exists in the understanding alone, the very being, than which nothing greater can be conceived, is one, than which a greater can be conceived." In other words, using (4), we have that

(e)((Ee_1)e_1 Cncv e,'Uns' $\supset$ (Ee')((e_1)(e_2)(e_3)((e_2 Des e_1 $\cdot$ Per e_1 $\cdot$ e_3 Des e') $\supset$ (Ee'')e_1 Able e'',$\ulcorner\langle e_2$,Cncv,e_3,'$\{e_4\ni$(Uns e_4 $\cdot$ E!e_4)$\}$'$\rangle$'$\urcorner$) $\cdot$ e' Gr e)).

"But obviously this is impossible," Anselm notes in conclusion, as indeed it is by (1''), (4), and (11). For by (1''), (A), and (4) we would have that

(Ee)(Uns e $\cdot$ (Ee')((-----) $\cdot$ e' Gr e)),

which runs afoul of (11). "Hence, there is no doubt that there exists a being, than which nothing greater can be conceived, and it exists both in the understanding and in reality." In other words

'(Ee)(Uns e $\cdot$ (e_1)(Per $e_1 \supset e_1$ Cncv e,'Uns') $\cdot$ E!e)'

is thought to be established beyond doubt. The argument is of course an enthymeme, (2) also being needed, (2) in turn being provable from (5) and (6).

8

Some commentators discern a second proof in *Proslogium III*, a modal proof in some sense, and contrast it with the first. It seems more natural, however, to regard *Proslogium III* as a continuation of the preceding chapter and to view its contents as helping to characterize the "proof" as a whole. *Proslogium III* presupposes *Proslogium II*, but serves to bring to light additional principles.

"And it [(ιe $\cdot$ Uns e)] assuredly exists so truly, that it cannot be conceived not to exist. For, it is possible to conceive of a being that cannot be conceived not to exist; and this is greater than one that can be conceived not to exist." Clearly this last sentence may be construed to state that

(14) $(Ee)((e_1)(\text{Per } e_1 \supset (Ee_3)(Ee_4)(Ee_5)(e_3 \text{ Des } e_1 \cdot e_4 \text{ Des } e \cdot e_1 \text{ Able } e_5, \ulcorner\langle e_3, \text{Cncv}, e_4, \text{'Uns'}\rangle\urcorner)) \cdot \sim (Ee_1)(Ee_5)(Ee_3)(Ee_4)(E_3 \text{ Des } e_1 \cdot e_4 \text{ Des } e \cdot \text{Per } e_1 \cdot e_1 \text{ Able } e_5, \ulcorner\langle e_3, \text{Cncv}, e_4, \text{'}\{e''\ni \sim E!e''\}\text{'}\rangle\urcorner\rangle) \cdot (e')((Ee_1)(Ee_5)(Ee_3)(Ee_4)(e_3 \text{ Des } e_1 \cdot e_4 \text{ Des } e' \cdot \text{Per } e_1 \cdot e_1 \text{ Able } e_5, \ulcorner\langle e_3, \text{Cncv}, e_4, \text{'}\{e''\ni \sim E!e''\}\text{'}\rangle\urcorner) \supset e \text{ Gr } e'))$.

It is interesting to observe that (14) is provable using *inter alia* the preceding principles needed for *Proslogium II*. Let 'e Eq e'' express that e is *equal in greatness to* e'. It is then assumed that

(15) $(e)(e')(e \text{ Eq } e' \text{ v } e \text{ Gr } e' \text{ v } e' \text{ Gr } e)$,

and hence

$(e)(e')((\text{Uns } e \cdot \sim e \text{ Gr } e') \supset (e \text{ Eq } e' \text{ v } e' \text{ Gr } e))$.

But clearly also

(16) $(e)(e')(e \text{ Eq } e' \supset (e_1 \text{ Gr } e \equiv e_1 \text{ Gr } e'))$,

and hence

$(e)(e')((\text{Uns } e \cdot e \text{ Eq } e') \supset \text{Uns } e')$,

by (10). Also by (2) and (13).

(17) $(e)(\text{Uns } e \supset \sim (Ee_1)(Ee_3)(Ee_4)(Ee_5)(e_3 \text{ Des } e_1 \cdot \text{Per } e_1 \cdot e_4 \text{ Des } e \cdot e_1 \text{ Able } e_5, \ulcorner\langle e_3, \text{Cncv}, e_4, \text{'}\{e''\ni \sim E!e''\}\rangle\urcorner))$.

And hence of course

$(e)(e')((\text{Uns } e \cdot e \text{ Eq } e') \supset \sim (Ee_1)(Ee_3)(Ee_4)(Ee_5)(e_3 \text{ Des } e_1 \cdot \text{Per } e_1 \cdot e_4 \text{ Des } e' \cdot e_1 \text{ Able } e_5, \ulcorner\langle e_3, \text{Cncv}, e_4, \text{'}\{e''\ni \sim E!e''\}\text{'}\rangle\urcorner))$.

Moreover,

$(e)(e')((\text{Uns } e \cdot e' \text{ Gr } e) \supset \text{-----})$,

because of (11). And hence in particular

$(e)(e')((\text{Uns } e \cdot e' \text{ Gr } e) \supset \sim (Ee_1)(Ee_3)(Ee_4)(Ee_5)(e_3 \text{ Des } e_1 \cdot \text{Per } e_1 \cdot e_4 \text{ Des } e' \cdot e_1 \text{ Able } e_5, \ulcorner\langle e_3, \text{Cncv}, e_4, \text{'}\{e''\ni \sim E! e''\}\text{'}\rangle\urcorner))$.

But now, by bringing these last threads together, we have that

$(e)(\text{Uns } e \supset (e')((Ee_1)(Ee_3)(Ee_4)(Ee_5)(e_3 \text{ Des } e_1 \cdot e_4 \text{ Des } e' \cdot \text{Per } e_1 \cdot e_1 \text{ Able } e_5, \text{'}\ulcorner\langle e_3, \text{Cncv}, e_4, \{e''\ni \sim E!e''\}\text{'}\rangle\urcorner) \supset (\sim e \text{ Eq } e' \cdot \sim e' \text{ Gr } e))$.

And hence, in view of (1''), (4), (17), (15), and (6), we get (14) itself.

Hence, Anselm concludes, "if that, than which nothing greater can be conceived, can be conceived not to exist, it is not then that, than which nothing greater can be conceived." In other words

$(e)((\text{Uns } e \cdot (Ee_1)(Ee_3)(Ee_4)(Ee_5)(e_3 \text{ Des } e_1 \cdot e_4 \text{ Des } e \cdot \text{Per } e_1 \cdot e_1 \text{ Able } e_5, \ulcorner\langle e_3, \text{Cncv}, e_4, \text{'}\{e''\ni \sim E!e''\}\rangle\urcorner)) \supset \sim \text{Uns } e)$.

This clearly violates (17) above. The argument of *Proslogium III* is thus also enthymematic, needing not only the principles of *Proslogium II* but also (15) and (16) as well.

9

Time, space, and energy permitting, it would be of interest to explore the remainder of the entire *corpus* for additional principles to round out this portrayal or "rational reconstruction" of the Anselmic setting. Enough has been shown, however, to suggest that this could very likely be done on the basis of the foregoing. Whatever the short-comings of this latter may be, it apparently is the most thorough portrayal of that setting on the basis of modern logic and semantics that has yet been given.

It should be noted that this portrayal could not be given within any logical framework lacking certain crucial features. First, a way of handling existence by means of a suitable predicate is needed, not just in the form of *Principia Mathematica*, *14.02, for descriptions, but in the form

$$\text{'E}!e\text{'}$$

for variable 'e'. The semantical truth predicate must be available, so that the theory must incorporate a semantical metalanguage. Further a way of handling intentional predicates such as 'Cncv' and 'Able' must be available, the method here being that of using the Fregean *Arten des Gegebenseins*, or modes of description. Finally, event-descriptive predicates must be available enabling us to handle acts (or events or states) of conceiving, in addition to all else. The total theory needed thus cannot consist of less than the entirety of event logic.

Perhaps other, more adequate, portrayals can be given on the basis of other types of logical system, but this seems never to have been done. Some writers insist upon reading modal concepts into Anselm, particularly into *Proslogium* III. These do not seem needed, however, and may well serve to distort rather than clarify. In particular, then, there seems to be no evidence at all that modal — or in general deviant — logics will be of service here in any way.

In what sense is the content of *Proslogium* III modal? Surely not in the sense of requiring modal logic, but only in the sense of being couched in terms such as 'possible to conceive', 'can be conceived', 'cannot be conceived', and so on. But these terms are not modal but dispositional and can be handled as above by means of the predicates 'Able' and 'Cncv'.

It is interesting that Desmond Henry, in this otherwise valuable study, argues for the use of modal notions in *Proslogium* III by omitting the key term 'cogitari' in order to give a "literal" translation. That, in *Proslogium* III, "we are now in the region of the Anselmian modal complex is clear, since three modal expressions, formerly veiled by the interposition of 'to-be-thought' (*'cogitari'*) ... have now been made explicit : (i) 'not possible not to be', (ii) 'possible to be', and (iii) 'possible not to be'."[5] To omit the key term 'cogitari' from *Proslogium* III, however, it would seem, is to distort its content beyond recognition. We cannot omit 'cogitari' and have the same text at all, nor the same logic accommodating it.

It might be objected that the foregoing "rational reconstruction" depends too heavily on modern logic. It is this latter that distorts, it might be argued, and any attempt at a reconstruction therefore should be based only on Anselm's logic. "The policy of assuming oneself to be ignorant of the author's understanding until one is certain that one has understood his ignorance is essential here [Henry, p. 250] as in all studies in the history of philosophy and logic." Yes, but one should not therewith confine oneself to his ignorance. History must continually be viewed and rewritten in the light of present knowledge, including of course that Socratic gadfly logic itself in its present form. The fact is that the really great achievements of the past do not crumble when so viewed, but stand up remarkably well.

Much further discussion is needed concerning 'Able' and 'Cncv', two of the key notions required in the above. It might well turn out that the principles governing these needed for the ontological argument would not be acceptable to modern ears. Anselm's logic of concepts may not be the same as ours. Also the predicate 'Gr' had for the medieval mind a very different meaning than it may have for us. Thus the best we can hope for, in a study such as the present, is to exhibit clearly the linguistic forms allowed, the ultimate premisses, and the modes of inference. The question of the acceptability of the ultimate premisses will always be disputable.

To summarize. It is noted in this paper that

$$\text{'E!}(\iota e \cdot \text{Uns } e)\text{'}$$

is provable from (5), (6), (9), (10), (12), (13), standard semantics, and of course standard logic. The premisses are explicitly exhibited in terms of the linguistic forms allowed. This much seems to give essentially the content of *Proslogium* II. *Proslogium* III, on the other hand, purports in effect to establish (14) on the basis of (15) and (16)

---

[5] *Loc. cit.*, p. 146.

together with the material needed for *Proslogium* II. There is thus something genuinely new in *Proslogium* III, as shown by the need for (15) and (16) concerning 'Gr'.

It is hoped that the results of this paper, as well as of some of the foregoing ones, will help to convince the reader of the indispensability of the procedures of modern logic not only for philosophic analysis, metaphysics, and philosophical theology, to say nothing of the philosophy of mathematics, but for the deep study of the history of philosophy as well.

IX

ON BOCHEŃSKI'S LOGIC OF RELIGIOUS DISCOURSE

"QUI A MUCE NUCLEUM VULT, FRANGAT NUCEM."

The very phrase shocks. What indeed is a "logic of religious discourse" or a "logic of religion," let alone "*the* logic of religion."[1] But Father Bocheński seems glad to shock and to lead us to the portals of a "relatively unexplored field" of a highly general kind. Ultimately the aim would be "to formulate a general logic of religion applicable to all great religions rather than to a particular religion." But for the present, he says in effect, we must remain at the portals only and survey the general terrain.

The logic of religion is presumably a species of applied logic. Just what is applied logic and what in particular is an applied logic of religion? Father Bocheński's is no doubt the fullest answer to this last question that has been given to date. Even if it should turn out to be far from satisfactory, it merits a rather full discussion.

Father Bocheński is undoubtedly one of the most valuable contemporary writers on logic. He is after all thoroughly versed in the new logic and at the same time deeply and broadly concerned with the abiding problems of philosophy. Also he is singularly free of what may be referred to as the mathematical bias. Logic in our time has become so intimately associated with mathematics and mathematical methods as perhaps to lose its proper identity. In the mid-nineteenth century, in the hands of Peirce and Frege, it will be remembered, logic had to struggle to free itself from the algebraic model of Boole and earlier workers. Curiously enough. now in the late twentieth century, after a period of intensive development, logic must struggle again to free itself from the grip of those with only mathematical interests. The enormously broad, non-mathematical area to which logic is

---

[1] J. M. Bocheński, *The Logic of Religion* (New York University Press, New York : 1965).

fruitfully applicable, has been well recognized by Bocheński, And the attendant attitudes are so very different anyhow that it is astonishing that logicians and mathematicians should ever have been thought bed-fellows.

So free in fact is Bocheński of the mathematical bias that he apparently fails to note the place of *mathematical* logic in his list of sorts of studies called 'logic' (p. 2). Formal logic, semiotics, methodology, and philosophy of logic are all included. Perhaps mathematical logic is to be squeezed in under one or more of these headings. Thus formal logic itself might be taken to include axiomatic set theory, but the view that it does is becoming somewhat unpopular.[2] Also semiotic might be thought to include the syntax, semantics, and pragmatics of mathematical languages. Nonetheless, because of its highly special character, it might be well to list mathematical logic, including metamathematics, foundations of mathematics, and the like, as a separate field of study.

At any event, *general logic*, according to Bocheński, includes formal logic, semiotics, and methodology, and has two outstanding characteristics : it is concerned (a) with discourse and (b) with "objective structures." As to (a), Bocheński's remarks are admirable and merit quotation in full. "In the whole history of logic, formal or otherwise," he writes (pp. 3-4), "there is no known case of any serious study which has not been carried out on the basis of some discourse. It is true that some philosophers (especially since Descartes) have talked about the study of concepts ...; however, logicians have always dealt with concepts as expressed by words, that is, with discourse. This tradition started with Plato and is still absolutely general. There seem to be two principal reasons for adopting this method. (1) Concepts do not subsist in themselves ... but are meanings of terms; therefore, they should be studied through the terms, that is, through discourse. (2) Written (or spoken) terms are material things (or events) — and it is a basic methodological principle that, whenever it is possible, we should start with such things (or events), because they are much easier to study than mental entities."

Some contemporary logicians, notably Church, call those whose interest is in discourse 'nominalists', and in fact the term is frequently

---

[2] See especially W. V. Quine, *Set Theory and Its Logic* (The Belknap Press of Harvard University Press, Cambridge : 1963) and cf. Martin Davis, "First-order, Second-order and Higher-order Logic," an address before the Association for Symbolic Logic, December 27, 1963.

used in this rather broad sense. But this is surely not a happy use, for the logician interested in discourse need not be interested in discourse exclusively. He may *quā* semanticist be interested in non-linguistic objects, including abstract ones, as well. And if, as Bocheński urges (p. 4), "in practice he [the logician] always deals with discourse," then every logician is in practice a nominalist in Church's sense. This is surely not a welcome consequence for those who use 'nominalistic' in this very broad way.

Bocheński advises us, by way of a general methodological maxim, to start our investigation with written or spoken terms (material things or events), these being easier to study than mental entities. It is evident that Bocheński's maxim here is in favor of an inscriptional syntax and semantics, as opposed to a classical one based on sign designs or shapes. Oddly enough, however, inscriptional syntax and semantics have been developed only very recently. Classical syntax and semantics, which are based on sign designs, as a matter of historical fact, were formulated much earlier. Bocheński refers to the work of Tarski but makes no mention of the work on inscriptions, which the maxim extols. Nonetheless, there can be no doubt that syntax and semantics, whether based on inscriptions or shapes or both, are "easier" than the study of mental entities, and that a valuable approach to the latter is therefore via the former.

General logic is concerned, we are told, with "objective structures." "There is a practically unanimous consensus among logicians," we are reminded (p. 4), "that they are primarily dealing with some of the most general structures of objects, and not with subjective acts of the mind. ... For example, when a logician states that, if no A is B, then no B is A, ..., he is establishing a necessary connection between two states of things." Little more is said as to what these objective structures are, and it is doubtful that all logicians would recognize themselves in this description. A sentence of the form 'If no A is B then no B is A' where 'A' and 'B' are one-place predicate constants, may surely be described harmlessly as establishing a necessary connection between A and B. But it by no means follows from this that a necessary connection is therewith established between the ("states" of) objects having A and those having B. The sentence 'If no dogs are cats then no cats are dogs' establishes no "necessary connection" between any individual cat and any individual dog, or between states of such. Logicians are concerned surely with the logical form of statements, and these are objective structures in some sense. But to require that they are objective structures of objects is at best misleading.

Bocheński's notion of objective structure is used to state the fundamental "theorem" (p. 7) that "for all f, if f is a field of human activity, then there is applied logic of f if and only if f includes discourse which embodies or expresses some objective structures." This "theorem" is rather vague but no doubt succeeds in drawing attention to the almost universal applicability of logic.

Bocheński suggests that logicians do not deal with "subjective acts of the mind" and hence that such acts do not have an objective structure. This is doubtful. To be sure, logic has scarcely been applied to the study of such acts as yet. To get at their objective structure is not easy, but this is not to say that they have none.

Let us consider now what an applied logic of religion would be. An outstanding characteristic of religious behavior, we are told (p. 10), is the use of a particular language, called 'religious discourse' ('RD'), a non-empty subclass of the sentences of which is called 'the Creed'. The religious discourse is itself presumably a part of a natural language. The applied logic of religion will then consist mainly of the application of logic to the "empirically given" RD as it is actually used by religious communities.

A host of difficulties arises from these comments. RD contains presumably all manner of sentences other than declaratives : exhortations, commands, optatives, questions, perhaps exclamations: but logic has been almost exclusively to date confined to declaratives. How then can one even dream of a logic of religious discourse? Bocheński mentions in passing other types of logic, for example, modal logic, deontic logic, and Austin's theory of performatives. But none of these types, should they turn out to be legitimate, seems especially relevant to RD. Other types, not mentioned, seem more so, such as those concerned with questions, commands, beliefs, knowledge, and the like.

RD being a branch of natural language, the logic of RD would have to contain the logic of at least a part of natural language. And if RD is empirically given, its analysis would presumably make use of the technics of empirical or structural linguistics. Even making use of such technics, all that one would have as a result would be some empirical or structural linguistics of RD. The question as to how this is related to logic remains open. The study of the exact relationship between the notions of logic and corresponding notions in natural language has scarcely begun. And yet Bocheński's conception of the logic of religion seems to presuppose a fairly full development of such study.

In the establishment of a logic of religion, we are told (pp. 11-12), there will be two successive stages. "The first will consist of the application of such laws and rules of general logic as have already been constituted for general purposes. ... The second step will presumably consist of the developing of special logical — formal, semiotic, and methodological — tools, which may be needed for the ... analysis of RD." The first consists in laying down the usual general laws of logic (concerning truth functions and quantifiers) for the declarative sentences of RD. It is not clear, however, whereof the second consists. What are those special logical (formal, semiotical, and methodological) "tools" that are needed? Actually there has been a fairly extensive development of formal syntax, semantics, and pragmatics, which supply no doubt useful notions of wide applicability, but of these Bocheński makes no mention and it is not clear that he has them in mind. These "tools," however, including those of formal logic itself, have been developed primarily in connection with the study of formalized languages, and it is by no means clear that they can be extended without ado to the natural languages. This brings us at once to a fundamental difficulty with Bocheński's approach.

In answering the question "To what material should logic be applied?" Bocheński states (p. 12) that "this material must be the empirically given RD as it is, namely, the discourse factually used by religious communities. This is also the case with other departments of applied logic; for example, logic of biology does not deal with a discourse conceived *a priori* but with the empirically given discourse of biologists." Bocheński goes on to state that Tarski's semantic definition of truth is another instance, and that the avowed aim of such a definition is to supply one "which fits the meaning of the everyday 'true'. ..." Tarski's procedure in this regard Bocheński regards as "an ideal for every sort of applied logic and, in particular, for logic of religion" (p. 13).

In direct contradiction to this, it may be contended that the aims of applied logic are quite different and often quite contrary to the needs of ordinary language. In fact, what the actual usages of language are is of little concern to the logician. He is concerned rather with how best to establish *technically sound* usage. He is concerned that such usage be both formally correct in certain specified ways and materially adequate for such and such well-articulated purposes. Sometimes, although probably only rarely, what he does may even influence actual usage. Peirce recognized this when he wrote (3.704) that actual "language has its meaning modified in technical logical formulae as in other special kinds of discourse" in the particular sciences.

It seems doubtful that there can be an applied logic without a rather high degree of formalization. In fact, an applied logic is, by definition, a system containing, in addition to the logical words, a suitable array of non-logical individual, functional, and/or predicate constants for the subject matter at hand. Over and against such a clear-cut notion, some logicians have, to be sure, spoken of a "semiordinary" language, in which ordinary language is made somehow to conform to, or to be "regimented" by, the principles of logic. Such a militaristic conception of applied logic, however, already admits some degree of formalization. But it is not clear that Bocheński has even this in mind. RD is, after all, empirically given "as actually used by religious communities" and thus not regimented in accord with logical principles. On the other hand, these principles are supposed to hold somehow, their application, as noted, being the first stage in the establishment of a logic of religion.

Also it is rather extraordinary for Bocheński to extol Tarski's procedure as a paradigm of applied logic. To be sure, Tarski's *object* languages are fully formalized, but not his metalanguages, which are left rather intuitive as is customary in mathematical writing. Thus if Tarski's procedure is to be regarded as an "ideal for every sort of applied logic and, in particular, for logic of religion" (p. 13), the object language at least must be fully formalized. Presumably then in place of RD, actual religious discourse as used in a given community, we must have something quite different.

The same, *mutatis mutandis*, obtains for the logic of biology. Bocheński mentions (p. 6) the work of Woodger approvingly and as providing as instance of "applied logic in the proper meaning of the term." But here again, one must distinguish the object languages from the metalanguages. Woodger's object languages are formalized, his metalanguages are not. And, contrary to what Bocheński says, the logic of biology, in Woodger's sense anyhow, does not deal, directly at least, with the empirically given discourse of biologists.

Bocheński agrees that difficulties arise due to the lack of "extensive empirical research in RD and its use within different religious communities." But he does not regard this as a "fatal handicap." "In

order to perform an analysis of such an abstract character as that
used in logic of religion," he tells us (p. 12), "perhaps it will be sufficient to take into consideration some obvious and universally known
features of RD and of the current behavior of the believers." What
we might hope to do, in accord with this, then, would be to develop a
metalogic describing certain very broad features of religious languages,
but without worrying too deeply about the inner structure of those
languages themselves. This latter would involve extensive empirical
research and also some formalization. This metalogic would contain
not only a syntax and a semantics, but also presumably a pragmatics
in which behavior and acceptance are taken account of in some
fashion.

Bocheński contends (p. 16) that the "logic of religion is relatively
more relevant to theology than the logic of sciences is to the sciences."
Theology is, by definition, it is said (p. 14), "a study in which, along
with other axioms, at least one sentence is assumed which belongs to
a given creed and which is not sustained by persons other than the
believers ..." in that creed. But no such assumption is needed in order
to study the logic of religion. This needs, we are told, two
classes of assumptions : the class of general logical laws and rules,
and the class of "metalinguistic statements about the concretely
existing RD's." Some of these metalinguistic statements will be syntactical, some semantical, and some pragmatical. "For example,"
Bocheński states (p. 15), "the student of logic of religion has to assume
that the believers of one or another religion say that God is our father;
the latter sentence, and this only, is a characteristic assumption of
theology." Hence logic of religion is not apart of theology, Bocheński
says, but is somehow supplementary to it.

Among the metalinguistic statements about a given object language
are usually included translations of the axioms of the object language.
Such inclusion is fundamental to Tarski's method. (There are other
kinds of semantics that lack this feature, the so-called non-translational semantics, but it is presumably not this that Bocheński has
in mind.)[3] Where then are such axioms to be located? One such axiom
in a given theology might be to the effect that God is our father.
But if so, it would have to reappear as a translation axiom of the
metalanguage. The logician of religion, as well as the theologian,

---

[3] On non-translational semantics, see *Truth and Denotation*, Chapters VIII,
IX, and XII.

would thus have to assume this, according at least to the Tarski conception and contrary to what Bocheński says. In addition, of course, the logician might assume also a pragmatical statement that such and such persons accept or believe the statement that God is our father. The logic of a theology clearly includes more than the theology itself, but merely because the pragmatical metalanguage includes modes of locution and principles not to be found in the object language. Meta-theology must transcend theology itself. Bocheński is essentially correct in this, it would seem, but does not apparently give an adequate reason.

Conversely, theology is clearly a part of the logic of religion, at least if the latter is taken as involving a translational semantics of the usual kind.

Of course one can study a system, at the semantical and pragmatical level, without being committed to belief in the axioms of that system. One can presumably study Zermelo's set theory, for example, without believing the axioms. One can admire Plato's vision of a realm of ideas without believing in it. One would be somewhat limited in proving metatheorems, however, without the object-language axioms. The device of taking these as antecedents or hypotheses where needed suggests itself. This would be similar to Russell's well-known dodge- (in *Principia Mathematica*) with regard to the axiom of infinity and the multiplicative axiom. Rather than to assume them outright, they are taken as hypotheses for the theorems which depend upon them. The logician of theology could take as hypotheses where needed such object-language axioms as he does not choose to assume.

If Bocheński really means that the logic of religion should include just the two classes of statements (general logical laws and metalinguistic principles) there are these two ways of accommodating the so-called translational axioms, via non-translational semantics or by taking them as hypotheses where needed. Both entail a radical departure, however, from the Tarski kind of metalanguage.

Is Bocheński right in claiming that the logic of religion is more relevant to theology than the logic of science is to science? Logic of religion becomes of interest to the theologian when the latter starts "reflecting" upon his work, we are told, upon its methods, aims, and so on. Similarly for the logic of science for the scientist, as Bocheński states. "The difference is ...," he tells us (p. 16) "this : although the scientist is not bound by the nature of his study to reflect, the theologian may be said to be obliged to do so." Bocheński is not of course claiming here that scientists do not think, or think well, or that they are not reflective upon the subject matter of their sciences. He is saying rather that meta-science is not the same as science, and that the former includes quite different modes of thought from the latter. The cast of mind required in the two types of discipline is different. In the case of theology and logic of religion, he thinks, this is not the case. The very tenuousness of the subject matter forces one to a greater concern for the modes of locutions and inference used.

In *Truth and Denotation*, it was argued at some length that applied logic is of greater interest for philosophic analysis than it is for mathematics or theoretical science. This view is in accord with Bocheński's contention about theology. In less exact subjects, where the fundamental vocabulary is in doubt, to say nothing of the axioms, applied logic provides a helpful guide. Where the subject matter is relatively clearer, as in mathematics or theoretical physics, the use of exact tools may lead to nothing essentially new or interesting, except perhaps at the metamathematical or meta-physical level. In theology, on the other hand, interest attaches to work at both levels, that is, (1) in the attempt to be clearer as to the exact linguistic structure of the theological object language, and (2) in studying this language from a syntactical, semantical, or pragmatical point of view.

Let us consider now (as in Bocheński's Chapter II) a little more closely the problem as to whether an LR, a logic of religion, howsoever conceived, is possible. All the intricacies of Bocheński's thought, or its consequences, or what is suggested by it, cannot be commented on, but only a few items of especial interest.

There is such a thing as RD. But whether there is such a thing as LR, and if so what, is far from clear. That there is such a thing has often been denied. In the history of the relations between logic and religion, two trends may be distinguished, which Bocheński calls the "logical" and the "anti-logical." Petrus Damianus is a good example of the latter in his view of logic as the work of the Devil. But there is also abundant evidence of the contrary trend. Every great religion has had periods in its history in which the application of logic to it was considered not only legitimate but of paramount importance, for example, the religion of Islam since the ninth century, Christianity from the thirteenth to the fifteenth centuries, and of Buddhism in India between the sixth and eighth centuries.

One might wish to uphold the anti-logical tradition on grounds roughly as follows. Logic and religion are just too different, it might be thought, and never the twain should meet. Religion is a personal, subjective affair, "what one does with one's solitude" (in the famous phrase of Whitehead), whereas logic is presumably the paradigm case of the interpersonal and objective. In religion all is based on faith, in logic, all on proof and rigorous deduction. And so on and on, the argument would run.

Well, as Bocheński points out, this argument has at least the merit of showing that logic and religion are not the same human enterprise, which, however, has never been doubted anyhow. No one would seriously contend that one must consciously pursue logic in carrying on religious discourse. Similarly one need not consciously pursue logic in carrying on scientific discourse, but there is some logic implanted there all the same. So at best the anti-logical argument does not succeed in proving what it set out to. One is not therewith driven to the logical camp, however. One can still be sceptical as to the possibility of a logic of religious discourse, if he so chooses. Bocheński is not so sceptical, however, and goes on to consider various types of meaning and the way in which these are related to different ways of construing RD.

The term 'meaning' is not used here in a technical sense. Bocheński has in mind no Frege-, Church-, or Carnap-like theory of *Sinne* or intensions or anything of the sort. When he uses 'meaning' no "shudder" quotes are required to indicate despair that genuine clarity can ever be achieved concerning it. He uses the word broadly merely to distinguish meaningful discourse from nonsense. He follows the old Stoic line in dividing meaningful utterances into objective and subjective, the objective being further divisible into communicative and non-communicative, the communicative being either complete or incomplete, the complete being either propositional or other. This Stoic table of meanings Bocheński uses as a guide leading to the theories of religion that he thinks *a priori* possible, that is, possible on the basis of this theory of meaningful discourse. The six theories are : (1) the nonsense theory (the sentences of RD have no meaning at all), (2) the emotionalist theory (the meaning is purely emotional or relaxative), (3) the non-communicativist theory (the sentences have in some fashion non-communicable meaning), (4) the communicativist non-propositional theory (whatever is communicated is non-propositional), (5) the theory of incomplete meanings, and (6) the propositional theory ("at least some parts of RD are intended to mean propositions").

Many questions arise here, as to the acceptability of the Stoic table, its very meaning, its completeness or lack of it, its relation to modern semiotic. One would then have to determine whether Bocheński's division of theories of meaning for RD is the correct one, or the only one, or even a suitable one.

Bocheński rejects (1)-(5) as proper theories of religion, not, however, without some detailed argumentation. Let the niceties of his arguments be waived for the present. Even if we, or he, had succeeded in showing these theories inadequate in on way or another, one still would not have established (6), the theory of propositional content. All one would have done, should (1)-(5) have been shown *a priori* impossible, is to have shown the *a priori* possibility of (6). Not content with doing just this, Bocheński purports to "prove" the following "theorem" :

Some parts of the RD of every religion are intended by their users to express and assert propositions.

The proof is given as follows (p. 41) : "We see that many parts of RD have the grammatical form of indicative sentences, which normally are used to express propositions. Many among them, especially those which are parts of the Creed, are said to be believed by the respective believers. Now it is true that the term 'believe' may be interpreted in such a way that it is not necessary to admit that whatever one believes is a proposition. But the following test precludes all possibilities of doubt about the character of belief as used in RD. First, we ask a believer of [some religion] r if he believes a sentence P, which is part of the RD of r. He, of course, will say that he does. Then we ask him if he thinks that P is true. It seems that there can be no doubt about the answer : the believer will always answer that he does, and he thinks P to be true. But a formula can be true only if it means a proposition. Therefore, the believers think that some parts of RD express propositions. Therefore the theorem is true."

This "proof," it would seem, is fallacious. From
(i)   'X thinks that P is true',
and
(ii)   'If P is true then P means some proposition',
it does not follow that
(iii) 'X thinks P means some proposition'
holds. And even if one amends (ii) to
(ii') 'X thinks it true that if P is true then P means some proposition',
(iii) still does not follow. One needs an additional premiss, perhaps

something to the effect that X believes the rule *Modus Ponens*. Thus one might add (put loosely) :

(ii'') 'If X thinks that C and also that if C then D, then X thinks that D, for all C and D of the discourse at hand,.

From (i), (ii'), and (ii''), (iii) logically follows. But to state this "trivial truth" is far from stating Bocheński's "theorem." For all this tautology states is that if X thinks so and so and such and such, he then also thinks this or that also — provided he is rational. Note that (ii'') is a kind of restricted principle of rationality. It is eminently rational to believe *Modus Ponens*. One does not have to perhaps, but it is surely rational to do so.

One must conclude then that Bocheński has not established his fundamental "theorem." Hence he has not established (6) as any better off than (1)-(5), so far as concerns the possibility of a logic of religious discourse. He has not succeeded in showing that "there is in religion a discourse which is meaningful, communicative, and partly, at least, propositional."

Nonetheless, it might be argued, *some* users of RD satisfy (i), (ii'), (ii''), and hence (iii), for example, Bocheński himself, where RD is perhaps some suitable version of Thomism. Hence, for such a user, there is presumably a propositional discourse subject to logical rule.

That RD must be a formalized language, or at least a partially formalized one, is evident from the discussion of its inner structure. Where this inner structure is talked about in some detail (Chapter III), the ideal of formalized axiomatic systems is held up as a paragon for religious discourse. After a brief general discussion of the "formal structure of a discourse," it is stated that the structure of RD differs from that of the discourse of science in primarily two respects : the role of authority, and the relations of RD to other discourses. These will be examined in a moment.

In the logical analysis of science there are, Bocheński contends, two "virtual axiomatizations." "Every propositional discourse ... is structured in some way. It need not be — and often is not — [explicitly] axiomatized, that is, its different factors are not explicitly stated; but, nevertheless, some structure is always present. If this is overlooked, it is because we are so accustomed to applying its rules that we do not notice them" (p. 53). One can, presumably, always transform a virtual axiomatization into an explicit one. One would have as a result of such a transformation a rational reconstruction of the subject matter at hand.

Two kinds of virtual axiomatizations are to be distinguished (p. 56). "In the first ..., only experimental sentences (along with some mathematical laws) are axioms; in the second, on the contrary, these sentences are derived theorems, whereas some sentences which were derived in the first system are now axioms." This distinction is not drawn too clearly, but presumably in the first axiomatization some rules of *inductive* inference are included, whereas in the second they are not. In the first virtual axiomatization general laws or explanatory hypotheses are inductively inferred from experimental sentences, these latter containing presumably only observation predicates. In the second, experimental sentences are deductive consequences of general laws.

The distinction between the two kinds of virtual axiomatization Bocheński thinks important for theology and the logic of religion. "Man is constituted in such a way that he always tends to axiomatize his discourse; and the religious man in no exception in this respect" (pp. 62-3). Consider some class of object-linguistic sentences, call it 'ρ', which incorporate the "objective faith" of the users of some RD. The sentences of ρ are "what the believers directly believe; ... they are sentences which are assumed by the believer without ... proof" (p. 60). ρ-sentences play, Bocheński thinks, a role in the logic of RD similar to that of experimental sentences in the logic of science. In the first virtual axiomatization of RD, ρ-sentences will appear as axioms — not all of them perhaps. but at least some, the others then being derivable. "Such an axiomatization," Bocheński says, "is the field of what is called 'theology' ... in the strict meaning of the term" (p. 63). Is there also a second virtual axiomatization in theology as in science? In mathematics, there is only the second kind of axiomatization. "Theology is more like physics than like mathematics," Bocheński says (pp. 64-5), and "... the main task of the theologian is the axiomatization of objective faith and not the deducing of consequences from it." It is thus only the first kind of virtual axiomatization then that is relevant to theology.

Fascinating as these comments are, it is difficult to see how they can be made other than on the assumption of a rational reconstruction of RD.

The phrase 'virtual axiomatization' is felicitous. It calls attention to the circumstance that one often wishes to assume that a given field is suitably axiomatized but is not prepared therewith actually to give the axioms. One merely assumes that this may be done in order to get on with the task at hand. But there is also an attendant danger in making too much of a merely virtual axiomatization. One may be tempted to gloss over the difficulties of actually giving axioms, in a field perhaps where this has never been done. And the difficulties here are often formidable.

Two major differences between the logic of religion and that of science have been mentioned. Authority plays a considerable role in the former, in particular, that of the creed and of Scripture. Bocheński notes that, for many religions at least, there is a purely syntactical rule indicating which sentences are to be considered as elements of objective faith, that is as p-sentences. "... [In] practically all religions there is a rule which says that whatever is contained in the Scriptures or the creed of that religion belongs to the objective faith" (p. 60).

Secondly, the discourses of some sciences are constructed autonomously without taking other [wider] discourses into consideration. "A physicist, for example, does not need, while constructing his system, to take into consideration the everyday discourse he uses outside science" (p. 58). In the case of RD, however, the situation is different. RD depends in intimate ways upon the total discourse of its users and "cannot be disconnected and considered separately from the PD (profane discourse) of the same subject."

The word 'God', or its equivalent, plays an important role in most RD's. It may well be contended that every p-sentence refers either directly or indirectly to God, by ascribing to him some property or relation (p. 66). Whether this is the case or not, the logical syntax and semantics of 'God' should presumably play a correspondingly large role in the logic of religion. But curiously Bocheński says very little of its syntax and practically nothing of its semantics. Syntactically viewed, RD is similar to PD in containing nouns, adjectives, verbs, and so on. Hence, it is said, 'God' may be either a name or an abbreviation for a Russellian description, a phrase of the form 'the one object such that so and so'. One would presume that in a given RD, 'God' is one or the other, and for all users. But no. "The class of those who use 'God' may be roughly divided into two mutually exclusive subclasses : that of prophets who are the authors of the Scriptures and so on, and that of believers who are the users of RD but not its authors" (p. 66). The prophets, at least some of them, presumably have direct acquaintance of God, and hence for them 'God' is a proper name. For those who have no such direct acquaintance 'God' is to abbreviate a description. It must be allowed also that some who are not prophets have such direct acquaintance, so that what Bocheński really states here is that "the term 'God', as used by the bulk of today's believers, is a description." It is namely an abbreviation for '$(\iota x \cdot \Phi x)$' where in place of 'Φ' a complex predicate is inserted for the properties attributed to God by the creed concerned.

It seems that Bocheński is here discussing two quite separate matters. Syntactically viewed, an individual constant of a given language must be either a primitive proper name or introduced definitionally by means of a Russellian description. The question of who uses the language is beside the point. Epistemologically or pragmatically viewed, one and the same expression may come to be known or used, as it were, by different users in different ways. No matter how an individual constant comes to be used, it remains either a primitive or a descriptional abbreviation. Because prophets have direct acquaintance with God, it does not follow that for them 'God' is a primitive proper name. Nor need it be a descriptional abbreviation for those who have no such direct acquaintance. Syntactically viewed 'God' must be one or the other for all users. This is required by logical syntax, and is quite independent of epistemological matters concerning use or knowledge.

Let us reflect now a little further upon the presumed "meaning" of religious sentences.

The vocabulary of RD, we are told, is essentially that of PD. "RD is itself composed of terms which are all either terms of profane-discourse or are defined by using such terms" (p. 94). The main difference between RD and PD is that "RD is supposed by its users to be about a transcendent object — the OR [object of religion]." Now 'God' is presumably not a term of PD. If all the terms of RD are terms of PD, 'God' must be definable in RD descriptionally. (This does not quite agree with what has just been said about its being a proper name for prophets.) The key difference between the two kinds of discourse will then really have to focus upon the transcendent object OR, and in particular upon the semantics of 'God'. But on this, as has already been remarked, singularly little is said.

Semantics for Bocheński is hitched, curiously enough, to the theory of verification. "A sentence has meaning if and only if there is a method of verifying it," he echoes with the older positivists. But 'verification' here must be taken in a very wide sense if the possibility of verifying p-sentences is to be allowed. "This presupposes ... that the believer does not limit the possible ways of direct perception to sensuous or even to natural experiences. A thoroughly Humean view of knowledge seems, therefore, to be incompatible with the assumptions of the believer" (p. 106). Thus a kind of "supernatural verification" is allowed, an act of "intellectual vision." But whether such acts are in any way verificatory, in any usual meaning of that word, seems doubtful. If ρ-sentences are to be accepted as a result of acts of intellectual vision in some fashion, let it be so. Such vision, however, seems very different from verification as practiced in the sciences.

From the semantics of ρ-sentences, something is supposed to follow concerning the semantics of the words occurring in them. The key word here presumably is that designating or describing the OR. The OR is a "mysterious" entity, it is suggested, and a sentence P containing a word or description for it is mysterious in the sense that (p. 109) "P contains at least one term a such that a is used in P in a way only partly corresponding to the use of a in PD." This partial correspondence opens the door to either negative theology or to the doctrine of analogy.

Negative theology does not make RD meaningless but only asserts that the properties ascribed to OR must in some sense be negative. "It seems that no partisan of this view has ever made an attempt to formulate it in sufficiently precise terms" (p. 111). No clear or satisfactory account of what a negative property is, in the sense needed, seems ever to have been given. And even if it had, the theory would still be inadequate, Bocheński thinks, for one "cannot worship an entity of which he assumes only that no positive properties can be ascribed to it" (p. 114). "It seems a sheer impossibility to worship, that is, to value, an entity about which one is prepared to assume only that it ... [has negative properties]. Such an entity is, for the user, completely void. ... It could be, for example, the Devil ..." (p. 36). Negative theology must therefore be discarded, it seems, and no interest will attach to the further exploration of its logic.

The doctrine of analogy, Bocheński thinks, fares better, as one might expect. What is it that is analogous to what? A term as used in PD will be said to be *analogous* to the same term as used in RD under suitable circumstances. First, it seems that the term must be a *relational* term or predicate — at least this seems to be the conclusion of most serious writers on the subject. And it is usually the OR who is said to stand in the analogical relation. Bocheński considers the example 'God is our Father'. 'Father' designates in PD any one (p. 116) of "a set of relations studied by different sciences, in particular, by physiology, psychology, and sociology. But it seems difficult to admit that any of these relations holds of God or of any other transcendent OR." What is it that is common between the two kinds of use? Bocheński suggests that "formal properties of relations are," such as reflexivity, symmetry, transitivity, and the like.

The logic of analogy is a big subject by itself, which Bocheński only touches upon here. "The whole field merits far more attention than has usually been given it," and is probably a most fruitful subject for Thomistic meta-theology. It very quickly becomes rather technical and special, however, and therefore no more need be said about it here.[4]

The final topic is that of the "justification" of religious discourse, in particular, that of the ρ-sentences. By "justification" Bocheński means "the activity by which the acceptance of a (meaningful) sentence is justified." And in fact it becomes clear that methodology, the fourth branch of general logic, is primarily the study of justification. Bocheński borrows from Jevons and Lukasiewicz the doctrine that all reasoning is either deductive or reductive, the general schema for reduction being :

$$\text{If } p \text{ then } q, \text{ and } q; \text{ therefore } p,$$

the common textbook fallacy of affirming the consequence. Inductive reasoning is, according to this, just one special case of reduction.

Bocheński's comments concerning the roles of deduction, reduction, and insight in scientific method could be commented on at some length, but it would be beside the point to do so for present purposes. He has in mind the older positivists' conception. Occasionally he mentions the concept of probability, but only in passing. There is no mention of the recent work on inductive logic, subjective probability, statistical inference, decision theory, the metatheory of science, and the like. Nonetheless it is of real interest to try to connect as best one can method in theology with descriptions of method in the sciences, showing that there is much greater similarity than might be supposed.

At several places Bocheński suggests that justification of sentences in RD is always metalinguistic, whereas it is often object-linguistic in PD. By this he means merely that at least one of the premises used for the justification is a metalinguistic sentence. "In metalinguis-

---

[4] See, however, Bocheński's Appendix and his much-discussed earlier paper "On Analogy," in A. Menne, *Logico-Philosophical Studies* (Reidel, Dordrecht : 1962).

tic justification," he says, "the procedure usually takes the following course. First, it is established (by deduction, reduction, or insight) that, whenever a sentence P has a certain contextual property Φ, then P is true. Then it is assumed (again by proof or insight) that P possesses the property Φ. It is then — deductively — concluded that P is true" (p. 121). The contextual property required for RD is, as has already been suggested, that of being found in the creed or Scriptures. The metalinguistic statement is that every sentence found in the creed is true. But also there is the possible appeal to the human authority : whenever such and such a person A (*quā* authority) asserts a sentence P, then P is true.

For those who are willing to accept ρ-sentences on the basis of authority of some kind, the problem of justification scarcely arises. The sentences are accepted on "trust." To say that person X trusts authority A is to say that X believes (p. 123) (1) that "A knows the situation in the field in which A is an authority" and (2) "A speaks truthfully about the elements of that field to the subject" X. X's trust here need not be based on any reasoning, although it is not ruled out that it might.

For those who are not willing to accept ρ-sentences on trust, justification will have to take other forms. Here Bocheński outlines several theories, but there is always "a considerable difference between the certainty of the faith and even the highest probability which can be obtained by justification" (p. 145).

We cannot begin to do justice here to the various alternatives. The most interesting, theologically as well as meta-theologically, seems to be the so-called "theory of the religious hypothesis." According to this, the believer constructs a certain explanatory hypothesis, perhaps the conjunction of all ρ-sentences in the creed. This sentence, the religious hypothesis — curiously Bocheński does not call it 'RH' — then is used to "explain" his experiences. "Formally," it is said (p. 148), "the procedure by which the religious hypothesis is established is closely similar to that used in reductive sciences. The starting point is [a set of] experimentally established sentences. The hypothesis is of such a nature that they may be deduced from it; it permits predictions and can be verified by new experimental sentences deduced from it." Two differences should be noted between an RH and an explanatory law in a science. The class of experimentally established sentences used as a starting point in religion is much more comprehensive than in a science. "The religious hypothesis of a person seems ... based on all sentences accepted by him, on his total experience" (p. 149). Also sentences concerned with moral and aesthetic values are to be included. Just what the logic of such sentences consists of, however, is not too clear. "The logical structure of the reasoning used [concerning them] is practically unknown" (p. 153).

The procedure of setting up an RH is well described in Bocheński's own words (pp. 149-150) : "... at a certain time of his life the subject begins to think that, that if he does accept the ... [basic dogma] of a certain religion, then the whole of his experience will become organized and somewhat explained. This is what writers probably intend to say when they assert that ... [religion] 'gives a meaning to the world and to existence.' Logically this means that the religious hypothesis plays the role of an axiom out of which the remainder is thought to be deduced (with the help of other sentences, of course). After this hypothesis has been formulated, it is verified by considering other different experimental sentences accepted by the subject. ... This nature of the religious hypothesis explains two curious phenomena occurring in RD : on one hand, the difficulty of persuading another man of its truth, and on the other, its very solidity, that is, the difficulty of overthrowing it by falsification. The first phenomenon is explained by the fact that no two persons have the same total experience [nor perhaps the same values]; and, consequently, a hypothesis which seems to be quite plausible to one of them does not need to appear plausible to the other, that is, related to his experience. The difficulty in overthrowing a religious hypothesis by falsification is again explained by its extreme generality. It is a trivial truth that the more general an explanatory sentence is, the more falsification it can take without being overthrown. One must be very little instructed in the procedures of science to think that a dozen facts inconsistent with a great physical theory will lead automatically to its rejection. But the religious hypothesis seems to be far more general ... than even the most general scientific theory. Therefore, it is must more difficult to overthrow it. It can be done, of course, but there must be quite an amount of falsifying evidence."

If one should balk at taking an RH as an out-and-out axiom, one could instead take it as hypothesis where needed, the Russellian device already suggested in another context above. If certain facts of one's experience cannot be "explained" other than on the basis of some RH, one has two choices before him : reject the facts or take as hypothesis or axiom some suitable RH. Exactly similar alternatives continually arise in the sciences.

First-order logic is now almost universally regarded as the fundamental or nuclear form of logic. Other types, including various forms of metalogic, seem to presuppose it in one way or another. It is not clear that Bocheński has in mind primarily this kind of logic. It will do us no harm, however, for present purposes, to regard applied logic as merely applied first-order logic. One will not be distorting Bocheński's intent nor will one be limiting too severely the logical tools or forms admitted.

Of course, the difficulty of formulating an RH, of actually writing it down, is formidable. A deep look at the syntactic structure of RD *from close to* is needed. Precisely what predicate constants are required? Just what kinds of variables, quantifiers, and so on? Can a first-order logic be made to suffice? Elsewhere Bocheński has contended that higher-order quantifiers are needed only in the formal sciences, especially in mathematics, and in logic only as a foundation for mathematics. Mathematics plays no conspicuous role in theology surely, and the presumption therefore, is that first-order logic may be made to suffice. At two or three points Bocheński suggests that other forms of logic might be needed, modal logic, intensional logic, or the like. But these are just passing comments, and nowhere is any use made of the notions of such logics.

Also the question of the intersubjectivity of the RH arises. Bocheński has described the procedures of building up an RH for just one person. Of course the RH of one person might differ remarkably from that of another. But there also might be striking similarities. The p-sentences might be regarded as the solid core, as it were, extracted from the RH's of the various members of a religious community. At any rate, there might be much intersubjective agreement. Objective agreement might be regarded as a limiting case of intersubjective agreement, so that even objective agreement might be reached, concerning some p-sentences anyhow. No doubt this is the case with the bulk of Catholic believers.

Bocheński's book would no doubt have been improved with greater attention to recent work in formalized semantics, ontology, systematic pragmatics, and the like. Frequently throughout it is lamented that suitable logical tools for philosophic analysis have not been developed. Of course this is true to some extent, but the fact is that Bocheński does not use even those that have, in particular those concerned with such notions as truth, designation, analytic truth, acceptance, belief, performance, acts, events, and the like.

A final comment. To pursue the logic of such and such a field is not to pursue the field itself. The logician of such and such a field is often accused of trifling and he is condemned if he fails to make substantive contribution to the field itself. Such condemnation arises, it seems, however, from a confusion of *genres*. The task of the applied logician is to give coherency and order to a subject, and not to pursue the subject directly in its own terms. Bocheński himself reminds us (p. 135) "that it is not the business of logic as such to interfere with the work of ... [the] sciences, ... [nor of theology], except insofar as it may examine the correctness of their reasoning." Logic bakes no bread and it is a mistake to suppose that it does. It would be unjust therefore to condemn Bocheński if he fails to further theology in any substantive way, for his task here has been quite different.

There is in Father Bocheński's book much to admire and agree with, and much else to try to improve upon. Although it contains some inadequacies and errors, "grievous errors which all are wont to make," there can be no doubt but that it remains a pioneering work in its field and a major contribution to it.

X

ON GURWITSCH'S THEORY OF INTENTIONALITY

"SIC VOS NON VOBIS."

Gurwitsch's recent discussion of "Husserl's definition of conscious-ness in terms of its intentionality" as "a revolutionary innovation in the history of modern philosophy" is clear, precise, and suggestive.[1] It may be of interest to see how what seems to be essentially his account may be viewed in the light of recent work in systematic prag-matics, event logic, and the like. In this way, hopefully, some light may be shed on the underlying logical structure of the theory of intentionality.

Fundamental to the discussion is the distinction between a *noema* and a *noesis*. The noema or "content" is neither "a psychological event nor a material thing," it is "devoid of both spatiality and tempo-rality, and ... of causality," and is "an identifiable ideal entity" having "the same [ontic] status as meanings." A noesis, on the other hand, is an "act of consciousness," a particular event or occasion going on in the subject experiencing it, a "temporal psychological event." There are many species or kinds of both noemata and noeses depend-ing upon "the various manners of adumbrational appearance" or presentation. Each such manner is presumably a "mode of con-sciousness, like the modes of perception, memory, symbolic represen-tation, and so on."

How can this distinction between noemata and noeses be accom-modated within event logic? Perhaps without distortion somewhat roughly as follows. An act of consciousness is "related" to an *object* and also is the act of some *person*. Acts of consciousness do not inhabit thin air, so to speak, but are always acts of some person or other. No harm can arise surely from introducing the person explicitly

---

[1] Aaron Gurwitsch, "Towards a Theory of Intentionality," *Philosophy and Phenomenological Research* 30 (1970) : 354-367.

into the theory. The person is needed quite as much as the object. Acts of consciousness are "temporal psychological events" and thus some reference to time seems essential in handling them. The simplest way for the moment, perhaps, is merely to recognize times as legitimate entities and to incorporate into the theory some way of handling temporal flow. To do so merely serves to make explicit and precise the needed reference to time.

The suggestion now is that modes of consciousness be handled in terms of *triadic relations*. Let '$p R x,t$' express that person p bears the mode of consciousness R to object x at time t. If R is a suitable relation for perception, '$p R x,t$' would express that person p *perceives* object x at time t. If R is a suitable relation for memory, '$p R x,t$' would express that p *remembers* at time t the object x. And so on. An enumeration of the various modes of consciousness would determine the range of the relational variable 'R'. Perhaps there is only a finite number of modes of consciousness, in which case a specific relational constant could be introduced for each one. Otherwise the use of the variable 'R' here is convenient.

The object-as-perceived is something quite different from the object itself. The object-as-perceived may be something quite different from the object-as-remembered. The object-as-perceived-at-time-t_1 may be very different from the object-as-perceived-at-time-t_2. The object-as-perceived-by-person-p_1-at-time-t may be very different from the object-as-perceived-by-person-p_2-at-time-t. To handle these and similar notions, a notation is needed for 'object-x-as-perceived-by-person-p-at-time-t', or, more generally, for 'object-x-as-borne-the-mode-of-consciousness-R-by-person-p-at-time-t'. This may readily be provided by the use of ordered quadruples. Let

(1)   '$\langle p,R,x,t \rangle$' abbreviate '$\hat{p}_1\hat{R}_1\hat{x}_1\hat{t}_1(p_1 = p \cdot R_1 = R \cdot x_1 = x \cdot t_1 = t \cdot p_1 R x_1,t_1)$'.[2]

Noemata in general now may be handled as ordered quadruples of this kind. A notation for a specific noema is provided by replacing the variable 'R' here by a specific relational constant for some one mode of consciousness.

Note that noemata as thus conceived have some at least of the properties Gurwitsch requires of them. They are devoid of spatiality

---

[2] The notation is an extension of that of *Principia Mathematica*, *21.01.02, for a certain kind of quadratic relation. On ordered n-tuples as philosophic paradigms, see W. V. Quine, *Word and Object*, pp. 257 ff.

and temporality, being abstract ordered quadruples of the same status as sets or relations. Of course one factor of the quadruple is a spatial object and one a time, but this circumstance confers neither spatiality nor temporality upon the quadruples as such. Nor are quadruples of this kind suitable relata for a causal relation, at least not in any familiar sense. What are the proper relata of causal relations? This is of course a difficult question requiring separate discussion. One answer is : events or, better, events taken under a given linguistic description.[3] Further, noemata have essentially the same status as meanings, as abstract entities of some kind or other, if the latter are taken as intensions or suitable reconstructions of Fregean *Sinne* or the like. More will be said about this in a moment.

How now may noeses, which are psychological events or particular acts of consciousness, be handled? Perhaps in terms of event logic as follows. Where the expression

$$'\langle p,R,x,t \rangle'$$

is regarded as a predicate rather than a term,

(2) $'\langle p,R,x,t \rangle e'$

expresses that e is a person-p's-bearing-mode-of-consciousness-R-to-object-x-at-time-t event. There may be several such events or perhaps just one. The same noema may be realized in many different acts, although it is possible that in fact it is realized in just one. A noesis now is merely an e having such an event property, that is, an event partaking of a given noema, where partaking is merely the relation of e to $\langle p,R,x,t \rangle$ where $\langle p,R,x,t \rangle e$.

Some periphrasis is involved here in using both variables for events and for times, as noted already in II above. If one kind is used, presumably the other is not needed. We should be able surely to introduce times by definition in a suitably developed theory of events, or events in a suitably developed theory of time. Thus, let the time variables now be dropped. The definiendum of (1) becomes merely

$$'\langle p,R,x \rangle',$$

and expressions of this kind with constants replacing the variables, are now to be taken to stand for noemata. Thus (2) now becomes

(3) $'\langle p,R,x \rangle e'.$

Note that this change does not alter in any essential way the characteristics required of them.

---

[3] See Donald Davidson, "Causal Relations," *The Journal of Philosophy* 64 (1967), 691-713; *Logic, Language, and Metaphysics*, Chapter VIII; and *Events, Reference, and Logical Form*.

Gurwitsch's key point (p. 364) is that the "intentionality of consciousness denotes precisely the correspondence between acts as temporal psychological events and noemata as ideal atemporal entities. ... We thus arrive at the *conception of consciousness as a correlation between items pertaining to two entirely different planes* : ... More precisely, it is a many to one correlation because to an indefinite number of acts or noeses there may, and does, correspond an identical noema. Differently expressed, *consciousness proves to be indissolubly — for essential reasons — connected with sense and meaning.* To every act of consciousness there corresponds, though it is not included in it as a real part or ingredient, an intentional or noematic correlate, an *intentional object* defined as the *object or state of affairs which is intended, but taken exactly and only as it is intended.*"

This key passage seems to contain implicitly at least three principles. To state these two or three definitions will be helpful. Perhaps we can say that event or occasion e is an *R-intentional act by person p towards object x* if and only if $\langle p,R,x \rangle e$. Thus

'e $RIntnl_p$ x' abbreviates '$\langle p,R,x \rangle e$'.

Then p's R-consciousness may perhaps be regarded as the fusion, in the sense of the calculus of individuals, of all acts e that bear $RIntnl_p$ to some object or other.

'$RCnscns'p$' can abbreviate 'Fu'$\hat{e}(Ex)\langle p,R,x \rangle e$'.

Similarly, p's consciousness in general is the fusion of all of p's acts of consciousness.

'$Cnscns'p$' abbreviates 'Fu'$\hat{e}(ER)(Ex)\langle p,R,x \rangle e$'.

Finally, consciousness in general is the fusion of the class of all intentional acts.

'$Cnscns$' abbreviates 'Fu'$\hat{e}(Ep)(ER)(Ex)\langle p,R,x \rangle e$'.

These definitions part from Gurwitsch's account, but only incidentally. In place of speaking of an R-intentional act, we could speak of an R-conscious act. In place of speaking of p's R-consciousness, we could speak of p's R-intentionality. And so on. The use of 'consciousness' in these contexts seems a little more natural in English than 'intentionality'. (The use of fusions here is perhaps not essential. If so, the definientia could be taken as merely the expressions for the classes involved rather than for their fusions.) Also let

'$IntAct$ e' abbreviate '$(Ep)(ER)(Ex)\langle p,R,x \rangle e$',

so that e is an *intentional act*, a noesis, if and only if e is an $\langle p,R,x \rangle$ act for some p, some R, and some x.

The following principles now seem to obtain and are implicit in the passage cited.

(4) $(e)(\text{IntAct } e \supset (Ep)(Er)(Ex)\langle p,R,x\rangle e)$.

"To every act of consciousness there corresponds ... an intentional or noematic correlate, an *intentional correlate*, defined as the *object or state of affairs which is intended, but taken exactly and only as intended*."

(5) $(e)(\text{IntAct } e \supset (\sim (Ep)e = p \cdot \sim (ER)e = R \cdot \sim (Ex)e = x))$.

An act of consciousness is not identical with any real part or ingredient of any noema. (Note that for the statement of (5) '=' is assumed significant as between expressions for noeses and persons, noeses and relations, and noeses and objects.)

The following three principles lead up to a strong principle of correspondence but may first be stated separately.

(6a) $(e)(R)(p)(x)(q)((e \ R\text{Intnl}_p \ x \cdot e \ R\text{Intnl}_q \ x) \supset p = q)$.

(6b) $(e)(R)(p)(x)(S)((e \ R\text{Intnl}_p \ x \cdot e \ S\text{Intnl}_p \ x) \supset R = S)$.

(6c) $(e)(R)(p)(x)(y)((e \ R\text{Intnl}_p \ x \cdot e \ R\text{Intnl}_p \ y) \supset x = y)$.

From these three we gain the strong principle of correspondence, that an R-intensional act or noesis stands in a many-one correspondence (in the sense of *Principia Mathematica*, *71.02) to an identical noema.

(7) $(e)(R)(p)(x)(S)(q)(y)((e \ R\text{Intnl}_p \ x \cdot e \ S\text{Intnl}_q \ y) \supset (R = S \cdot p = q \cdot x = y))$.

Principle (7) is equivalent to the conjunction of (6a), (6b), and (6c), but it is not clear that all three of these should obtain, nor that Gurwitsch wishes to assert that they do.

(6a) surely is legitimate. An intensional act is presumably the act of one and only one person.

(6b) might obtain if we require that the various modes of consciousness are quite separate from one another, in no way overlap, and so on. If so, then no intentional act can be both an R-intensional act and an S-intensional one of the same person for the same object, for distinct R and S. No perception of x is a memory of x. No perception of x is a desiring of x, and so on. This seems a strong requirement, however, for modes of consciousness intermingle with each other in all manner of ways. Cannot one and the same complex act be simultaneously an act of perceiving, of memory, and of desiring? Or is any such complex act decomposable only into successive phases as it were, and not into simultaneous ones? Before we decide whether (6b) holds, this and similar questions must be answered.

And similarly for (6c). Must every intentional act be intended towards one and only one object? Can one not perceive two distinct objects in one and the same act? Can one not desire coffee and cream in one and the same act of desiring? And so on.

For the further development of the theory systematic ways of compounding acts, modes of consciousness, and objects among themselves seem needed. No doubt the calculus of individuals would be helpful here. Given two objects x and y there is then a compound object $(x \cup y)$ whose various atomic parts are just the stomic parts of x or y. If e bears $R\mathrm{Intnl}_p$ to x for suitable R, p, x and y, can it not also bear $R\mathrm{Intnl}_p$ to y or to the compound or sum individual $(x \cup y)$? Similarly, cannot the noeses themselves be compounded, in terms perhaps of their temporal succession? And no doubt the modes of consciousness also can be compounded in accord with the calculus of relations (*Principia Mathematica*, *23, but for triadic relations). These difficult matters we need not go into here, but would surely have to be settled in a full account of the theory.

Note that (4) above is merely a logical truth of the theory, but that (5) and (6a) are factual, perhaps suitable to be taken as axioms or postulates. The status of (6b), (6c), and hence (7), is left open.

Gurwitsch contends (p. 364) that "the identity of the noema ... cannot be explicitly disclosed unless the acts or noeses are at the same time rendered explicit in their temporality. Conversely ... no account of the temporality, especially the duration, of an act of consciousness is possible except with reference to the corresponding identical atemporal noema."[4] That there is no disclosure or realization of a noema other than in a noesis is built here into the very notation. The predicates '$\langle p,R,x \rangle$', and so on, are significant only with the event variables 'e', and so on, as arguments. The converse requirement is less obvious, but no doubt can be accommodated by laying down suitable principles interrelating the temporal flow of occasions with the intentional predicates. One way of handling temporal flow, just by itself, is in terms of a primitive *before-than* relation.

In addition to intentional acts, there are presumably all manner of non-intentional ones. To handle these the whole apparatus of event logic may be introduced. The variables 'e', and so on, then range over

---

[4] See also his "On the Intentionality of Consciousness," in *Philosophical Essays in Memory of Edmund Husserl*, ed. by M. Farber (Harvard University Press, Cambridge : 1940), or in A. Gurwitsch, *Studies in Phenomenology and Psychology* (Northwestern University Press, Evanston : 1966).

a wider domain of acts, states, events, occasions, and the like. With
this extension, the intentional predicates may now be construed
with event variables or names in place of the thing variables. Thus
'$\langle p,R,e \rangle$' may be significant where e is an event R-intended by p.
Person p may perceive the event of John's-kissing-Mary. However,
the question arises as to whether e here could itself be an intentional
act. If so, some modification of (2) must be made. But just how?
Gurwitsch claims that no act of consciousness is a real part or ingredient of any noema. This seems strong. Can one not remember that
one remembered something in the past? Can one not desire to perceive
something in the future? To allow a noesis to be an ingredient in a
noema, in the sense of being a factor in place of an object, seems
not unreasonable.

A word now about the ontic status of noemata as abstract objects
akin to meanings. "As usually understood," Gurwitsch notes (pp. 363-
4), "the term meaning is related to verbal or, more generally, symbolic
expressions. However, the term can be so generalized as to become
synonymous with the term 'sense' or noema. If it is thus generalized,
the term 'meaning' denotes an object or state of affairs of any kind,
as that object or state of affairs is meant and intended through a
certain act of consciousness, perceptual or other, as the object or
state of affairs presents itself to, and stands before, the experiencing
subject's mind. Meanings, in the narrower and proper sense, equivalent to signification, prove to form a special class of noemata or
meanings in the wider sense."[5]

It is interesting to compare this doctrine with some suggestions
concerning referential acts made in *Events, Reference, and Logical Form*.
Let 'Ref' stand for the relation of reference discussed there. Let 'a',
and so on, be syntactical variables for linguistic expressions. Then
(8)   '$\langle p,\text{Ref},a,x,b \rangle e$'
may be introduced to express that e is one of person p's acts — or
states, these need not be distinguished here — of referring to the object
x by means of the linguistic expression a as occurring in sentence b.
Referential acts are then linguistic acts of a certain kind and can be
handled very much as noeses are. One may then well contend that
linguistic acts constitute a subclass of noeses in general. Gurwitsch's
suggestion is the related one, however, in effect to handle the quadrup-

    [5] See also A. Gurwitsch, *The Field of Consciousness* (Duquesne University
Press, Pittsburgh : 1964).

les $\langle p$, Ref,$a,x,b \rangle$ very much as noemata. This is an interesting suggestion, although of course there is the crucial difference that in the
expressions for linguistic noemata, a linguistic factor is admitted
that is not needed in noemata proper, at least as handled above.
More on this, however, in a moment.

It may be questioned whether predicates of the form '$\langle p$, Ref,$a,x,b \rangle$'
represent meanings in any technical sense of the word yet put forward.
Of course $\langle p$, Ref,$a,x,b \rangle$ is like a noema in the following way. $\langle p,R,x \rangle$
can be thought of as the object-x-as-borne-R-by-p. Similarly $\langle p$,
Ref,$a,x,b \rangle$ can be thought of as the object-x-as-referred-to-by-p-by-
means-of-the expression-a-as-occurring-in-b. It is the object taken in
a given *Bestimmungsweise* or *Art des Gegebenseins* (Frege's phrases)
by person p. An object so taken may be thought of also as a conception
of that object. Conceptions so handled are in effect classes (or virtual
classes) of referential acts, just as noemata are in effect classes of
noeses.

Can *meanings* be introduced now technically as conceptions or as
classes of referential acts so as to have essentially the same ontic
status as noemata? It is intriguing to consider the following possibility, although it parts considerably from Husserl and Gurwitsch.
Person p's acts of referring to object x by means of predicate a may
or may not be linguistically correct ones. Linguistically correct usage
is given by the semantical rules of the language. The semantical rules
here are assumed to be couched in terms of multiple denotation, so
that 'a Den x' expresses primitively that a denotes x.[6] An act e may
then be said to be a *linguistically correct referential act (or state)
concerning predicate a* if and only if for some p, x, and b, e is a $\langle p$,
Ref,$a,x,b, \rangle$ act and also a Den x. Thus

'e LCRef a' abbreviates '$(Ep)(Ex)(Eb)(\langle p,$Ref,$a,x,b \rangle e \cdot a$ Den $x)$'.
The totality of p's linguistically correct referential acts or states concerning a is an interesting class concerning p and his linguistic behavior,
but it would not be a class revelatory of the meaning of a.

On the other hand, the totality of linguistically correct acts concerning predicates b logically entailed by a would be revelatory of the
meaning of a, in the sense of 'meaning' akin to the traditional connotation or comprehension of a. The expressions a and b here are one-
place predicates in accord with the theory of multiple denotation.
Let 'a LImp b' express that the one-place predicate a logically implies

[6] As in *Truth and Denotation*, Chapter IV.

or entails the one-place predicate b. This notion is definable in terms of the notion of analytic or logical truth, itself definable in the underlying semantics.

Consider now the totality of linguistically correct referential acts concerning predicates b L-implied by the predicate a. Such a totality may, in accord with the present account, be regarded as the meaning of a. If so,

'm(a)' may abbreviate '$\hat{e}$(Eb)(a LImp b · e LCRef b)'.

Meanings as thus conceived have the same status as noemata, as classes of noeses. They are akin to the traditional notion of the connotation or comprehension of terms. And further, they embody implicitly the Fregean *Arten des Gegebenseins* in the sense that each member of a meaning is a denotational act of taking an object in a given *Art des Gegebenseins*.

There are of course many kinds of linguistic acts other than referential ones : apprehension acts, acceptance acts, rejection ones, utterance ones, assertion ones, question ones, commands, exclamations — to mention only a few of the most important. Each of these requires a separate study prior to attempting to formulate an integrated theory. A similar comment no doubt may justifiably be made concerning the various types of noeses in general.

Linguistic expressions in the foregoing have been construed as sign designs rather than as sign events. Presumably with only slight changes, however, sign events could be used instead. Note also that most of the foregoing can be accommodated on the basis of a first-order logic (although actually a one-sorted set theory has been used, with the convenience, however, of different styles of variables). At a few places a quantifier over intentional relations has occurred. With an explicit enumeration — if such can be given — of the modes of intentionality, these quantifiers could be eliminated. The use of the theory of virtual classes and relations would then presumably suffice.

The discussion of meaning suggests now that the foregoing account of noemata may be revised to take account also of the *Arten des Gegebenseins*. Noemata would then be more intensional (with an 's') in the semantical sense. Let us include now a linguistic factor in noemata. Let

(9)   '$\langle p,R,a,x \rangle e$'

express that e is one of p's acts of R-intending x *under the linguistic description given by the one-place predicate a*. In this way the noemata are made more intensional and construed rather more as meanings are.

Consider an example, like the one due to Elizabeth Anscombe. Person p may desire to meet the former President of the United States but have no desire to meet Mr. Richard M. Nixon. He thus desires to meet a certain person q under the description 'is the present President of the United States' but *not* to meet q under the description 'is identical with Mr. Richard M. Nixon'. Differences in intension are given here by differences in the *Arten des Gegebenseins*. The use of (9) in place now of (3) protects the theory from the charge of not being able to handle differences in intension in some suitable fashion. The resulting theory is also more unified than the preceding one, for (8) becomes now merely a special case of (9) with the constant 'Ref' put in place of the variable 'R'.

A merit of these considerations is that intentions (with a 't') and intensions (with an 's') are interrelated here in a logically clear and most intimate way. Many details of course remain to be supplied and some of the comments are mere suggestions. Even so, surely some progress has been made here in clarifying the purely logical structure of a theory of intentionality closely akin to that of Gurwitsch.